OUR LADY
of the
CONQUEST

OUR LADY
of the
CONQUEST

by
Fray Angélico Chávez

New Foreword
by
Marc Simmons

SOUTHWEST HERITAGE SERIES

SUNSTONE PRESS

SANTA FE

Sunstone books may be purchased for educational, business, or sales promotional use. For information please write: Special Markets Department, Sunstone Press, P.O. Box 2321, Santa Fe, New Mexico 87504-2321.

Library of Congress Cataloging-in-Publication Data

Chavez, Angelico, 1910-1996.
Our Lady of the Conquest / by Angélico Chávez ; new foreword by Marc Simmons.
    p. cm. -- (Southwest heritage series)
Originallly published: With new foreword. Santa Fe : Historical Society of New Mexico, 1948.
ISBN 978-0-86534-747-2 (softcover)
1. Conquistadora. 2. Cathedral of San Francisco de Asis (Santa Fe, N.M.)--History. 3. Catholic Church--New Mexico--Santa Fe--History. 4. Santa Fe (N.M.)--Church history. I. Title.
BT660.S45C5 2010
246'.960978956--dc22
                                    2009047817

Published in

WWW.SUNSTONEPRESS.COM
SUNSTONE PRESS / POST OFFICE BOX 2321 / SANTA FE, NM 87504-2321 /USA
(505) 988-4418 / ORDERS ONLY (800) 243-5644 / FAX (505) 988-1025

CONTENTS

SOUTHWEST HERITAGE SERIES

I

THE SOUTHWEST HERITAGE SERIES

"The past is not dead. In fact, it's not even past."
—William Faulkner, *Requiem for a Nun*

The history of the United States is written in hundreds of regional histories and literary works. Those letters, essays, memoirs, biographies and even collections of fiction are often first-hand accounts by people who wanted to memorialize an event, a person or simply record for posterity the concerns and issues of the times. Many of these accounts have been lost, destroyed or overlooked. Some are in private or public collections but deemed to be in too fragile condition to permit handling by contemporary readers and researchers.

However, now with the application of twenty-first century technology, nineteenth and twentieth century material can be reprinted and made accessible to the general public. These early writings are the DNA of our history and culture and are essential to understanding the present in terms of the past.

The Southwest Heritage Series is a form of literary preservation. Heritage by definition implies legacy and these early works are our legacy from those who have gone before us. To properly present and preserve that legacy, no changes in style or contents have been made. The material reprinted stands on its own as it first appeared. The point of view is that of the author and the era in which he or she lived. We would not expect photographs of people from the past to be re-imaged with modern clothes, hair styles and backgrounds. We should not, therefore, expect their ideas and personal philosophies to reflect our modern concepts.

Remember, reading their words and sharing their thoughts is a passport back into understanding how the past was shaped and how it influenced today's world.

Our hope is that new access to these older books will provide readers with a challenging and exciting experience.

Fray Angélico Chávez

II

FOREWORD TO THIS EDITION
by
Marc Simmons

He has been called a renaissance man and New Mexico's fore-most twentieth-century humanist by biographer Ellen McCracken. Any way you measure his career, Fray Angélico Chávez was an unexpected phenomenon in the wide and sunlit land of the American Southwest.

His life, which began at Wagon Mound, New Mexico in 1910, was filled with vigorous physical and intellectual activity. Above all, Fray Angélico was an independent and original thinker, traits not usually as-sociated with someone in a religious order who takes a vow of humility.

In the decades following his ordination as a Franciscan priest in 1937, Chávez performed the difficult duties of an isolated backcountry pastor. His assignments included Hispanic villages and Indian pueblos. As an army chaplain in World War II, he accompanied troops in bloody landings on Pacific islands, claiming afterwards that because of his small stature, Japanese bullets always missed him.

In time despite heavy clerical duties, Fray Angélico managed to become an author of note, as well as something of an artist and mural-ist. Upon all of his endeavors, one finds, understandably, the imprint of his religious perspective. During nearly seventy years of writing, he published almost two dozen books. Among them were novels, essays, poetry, biographies, and histories. Sunstone Press is now bringing back into print some of the rare titles.

Upon his death in 1996, Chávez left his huge collection of docu-ments and personal papers to Santa Fe's Palace of the Governor's His-tory Library, one of the region's major research institutions. In that year, it was renamed the Fray Angélico Chávez Library and Photographic Ar-chives.

Today, a handsome life-size statue of the padre in his Franciscan robe stands in front of the building on Washington Avenue. During the first severe winter after its unveiling, a good Samaritan placed a stocking cap on the head of the statue.

Throughout his life, Fray Angélico remained a confirmed Hispanophile. In the 1960s and 1970s, that stance won him the enmity of Chicano Activists, who rejected the Spanish side of their heritage. But Fray Angélico had spent too many years documenting the colonial record of New Mexicans' achievements on this far-flung frontier to succumb to the blandishments of anti-Spanish ideologues.

Indeed, of the many accolades he received in his lifetime, none pleased him more than the one bestowed upon him by Spain's King Juan Carlos: membership in the knightly Order of Isabel la Católica, granted in recognition of his contributions to learning and the arts.

All true aficionado's of the American Southwest's history and culture will profit by collecting and reading the significant body of work left to us by the remarkable Fray Angélico Chávez.

III

PREFACE
by The Rev. Msgr. Jerome J. Martinez y Alire, J.C.L.
Rector, Cathedral Basilica of St. Francis of Assisi
and Spiritual Director of La Cofradia de La Conquistadora

The Cathedral Basilica of St. Francis of Assisi
131 Cathedral Place, Santa Fe, New Mexico 87501
Parish founded in 1610
Church established as a Cathedral in 1853
Elevated to Basilica in 2005

PREFACE

Fray Angelico Chavez' "Our Lady of the Conquest," first published in 1948, is as timely now as ever. It details the origins and development of America's oldest devotion to the Virgin Mary in a scholarly yet devout manner. Chavez' account is at the same time eminently readable.

It will provide the reader with not only valuable history, but a greater appreciation of the faith of the Virgin's many adherents passed on from one age to another.

As Mary herself said in the Gospel of Luke 1,48, "all generations will call me blessed."

The Rev. Msgr. Jerome J. Martinez y Alire, J.C.L.
Rector, Cathedral Basilica of St. Francis of Assisi
and Spiritual Director of La Cofradia de
La Conquistadora

June 24, 2009, Feast of the Birth of
St. John the Baptist

P.O. Box 2127, Santa Fe, NM 87504-2127 Phone 505-982-5619 FAX 505-989-1952

IV

FACSIMILE OF 1948 EDITION

OUR LADY OF THE CONQUEST

Our Lady of the Conquest (La Conquistadora) in one of her several
dresses. This photograph was taken in the Rosario Chapel,
June, 1948, during her eight-day sojourn there

OUR LADY

of the

CONQUEST

Fray Angelico Chavez

THE HISTORICAL SOCIETY OF NEW MEXICO
SANTA FE   .   .   .   1948

Reprinted from Volume XXIII of
The New Mexico Historical Review

CONTENTS

ILLUSTRATIONS

FOREWORD

All who sincerely love the Southwest and its colorful history will concur with us in congratulating and blessing Dr. Sylvanus G. Morley for raising this true story of *Our Lady of the Conquest* from the relative obscurity of strictly historical pages into a beautiful volume that will attract the eye of all and sundry. For, perhaps more than any other single study on New Mexico life and customs, this work reproduces the very soul of the Spanish Southwest, and of our New Mexico in particular, by virtue of the very subject of which it treats — *"Nuestra Señora La Conquistadora."* This *Our Lady of the Conquest* means much more than the ancient little image treasured for so long in our Cathedral of Santa Fe; it means the spirit of deep-rooted Faith and Devotion which characterized the *Conquistadores* of this land, no matter what their individual or collective faults, a spirit which united all alike, regardless of class or station, in conquering an enchanting but indomitable region because they themselves had been conquered by the grace and beauty of "our tainted nature's solitary boast," she whom Don Diego de Vargas, the great *Reconquistador,* referred to as the "Queen and Patroness of this Kingdom of New Mexico and its Villa of the Holy Faith."

May this knowledge not merely aid us toward a fuller understanding of our land's wonderful history of three centuries and a half, but also assist us in the bettering of human relations beneath the mantle of all that is good and beautiful.

The author merits the praise and gratitude of all lovers of history and true civilization. We of the Southwest owe him a tribute of devoted appreciation for shedding more light upon the grand past of a region of which Santa Fe is the heart and inspiration.

+Edwin V. Byrne

ARCHBISHOP OF SANTA FE

OUR LADY OF THE CONQUEST

By FRAY ANGELICO CHAVEZ

INTRODUCTION

The centuries-old New Mexican Devotion of *Nuestra Señora del Rosario,* also called with affectionate familiarity *"La Conquistadora,"* deserves special study, not only because it parallels and perhaps exceeds three full centuries of Southwestern history, touching on important names and events at different periods, but also because, largely independent of official Church or State acts, it was a popular movement which brought the scattered Hispanic colonists of the Southwest together without regard to class or station. It was Spanish in concept and feeling, as contrasted with the primary concern of the Mission fathers with the Indians; and it was Catholic to the core, being founded on, and quickened by, an especially Spanish-Catholic filial devotion towards the Mother of God. Its main object was to honor Mary under the special title of "Our Lady of the Rosary" and, more particularly, as the "Lady-Conqueror" for ethnic reasons to be discussed later on. Officially, the royal government had nothing to do with the society and its activities, although the Governor as a private citizen often headed the list of civilian and military devotees from the entire "Kingdom." Even the Church, although all activities of the Confraternity centered entirely around religious functions under her supervision, did not include them in her ordinary official acts. In its early phase the Franciscan Fathers themselves enrolled and paid dues with the rank and file of lay-members, and only laymen were periodically elected *Mayordomos* and deputies. These facts explain, moreover, why no specific mention of the Confraternity is to be found in the civil and ecclesiastical acts of the Governors, *Cabildos,* and Franciscan *Custodios* of the seventeenth and eighteenth centuries; they also show why little or nothing was known in modern times about its nature and origin, except for clouded tradi-

1

tion and the annual event celebrated in Santa Fe from time immemorial which came to be known as the "De Vargas Procession."

Briefly, the popular tradition of the past century and a half is this: As the Spaniards were preparing to reconquer Santa Fe in 1692, the great Captain-General, Don Diego de Vargas, solemnly vowed to build a special chapel for his own favorite statue of Our Lady of the Rosary, should he gain a quick victory, and also to hold a yearly procession in her honor; the image was carried into battle and the Spaniards gained an effective *conquista*, and thereafter this particular image came to be known as *La Conquistadora* and Santa Fe's very own little Lady.[1] Other legends and practices grew around these bare essentials of the story. But decades ago our own Catholic historian, Benjamin Read, with all his warm devotion to things Spanish-American and his deep Catholic faith, could not accept it in the light of the de Vargas *Campaign Journals*, which make no mention of it at all, and because of the people's ignorance of two separate reconquests (1692 and 1693) by the same man.[2] Others have tried, in all sincerity, to evaluate the historic essentials of the tradition and to draw the best plausible conclusions therefrom, but they have been baffled by a complete lack of early historical sources.[3]

1. Very Rev. James H. DeFouri, *Historical Sketch of the Catholic Church in New Mexico* (San Francisco, 1887), p. 15. The author expresses this tradition as he learned it from the people of his day. See also Hallenbeck and Williams, *Legends of the Spanish Southwest* (Glendale, 1938), pp. 97-100, in which a chapter, entitled "La Conquistadora," treats the matter most sympathetically as a legend.

2. *Illustrated History of New Mexico* (Santa Fé, 1912), p. 293, note.

3. L. Bradford Prince, *Spanish Mission Churches of New Mexico* (Cedar Rapids, 1915), pp. 107-109. The author gives Father DeFouri's rendering of the popular version of the old tradition, and comments thus: "Matters of tradition can scarcely be expected to possess strict historical accuracy, and in the course of years dates which depend on human memory are likely to become uncertain, so it is not surprising that there are doubts as to the entire correctness of the foundation for this annual procession as stated by Father DeFouri." He then quotes Read's footnote and continues with greater insight and patience: "On the other hand it is difficult to conceive how a custom and tradition involving the whole community could have originated without some foundation."

One special article which treats the tradition *ex professo* is a study made over ten years ago by J. Manuel Espinosa, "The Virgin of the Reconquest of New Mexico," *Mid-America*, VII (1936), pp. 79-87. After quoting de Vargas about leaving for Santa Fe "under the protection of Our Lady of the Conquest" and his plans of restoring the old church for the same Lady, the author reiterates the popular tradition plus other legends and contemporary information acquired from old-timers in

The recent discovery of late seventeenth and early eighteenth-century fragments bearing directly upon *Nuestra Señora del Rosario La Conquistadora*, under this specific name, together with a fresh examination of early parochial records and the de Vargas *Campaign Journals* themselves, have made the present study possible. So many and so varied are the facets of this subject that it becomes necessary to treat the principal ones separately, closely interrelated though they be. The origin and nature of the *cultus* and its *hermandad* come first, for chronological reasons; then the *little statue itself*, the material object around which the devotion has revolved; and lastly, the question of *chapels*, and the annual *fiestas and processions*.

Santa Fe, and then draws out a complete and direct relation between particulars of the Santa Fe tradition and similar ones of a like tradition in Mexico City dating from Cortés. He then shows that the "Lady" of the 1692 peaceful reconquest was not a statue but the Royal Standard bearing a picture of Our Lady of *Remedios*, and that in the second entry of 1693, although the *Remedios* title is not used (only *N. S. de la Conquista*), both titles refer to the same image since in the Cortés tradition the titles are synonymous. Furthermore, the names *del Rosario* and *Conquistadora* are not to be found in old sources and, therefore, "On these grounds the conclusion would be that the present image of *la Conquistadora* is not the original one brought by Governor Vargas in 1693, or else that it was converted into a *Virgen del Rosario* sometime since reconquest days."

CHAPTER I

THE CULTUS AND CONFRATERNITY

D RIVEN out of their homes by the Pueblo Indian Revolt of
1680, the Spanish inhabitants of "*el Reyno de la Nueba
Mexico*" took refuge far to the south in the el Paso del Norte
district on the banks of the Rio Grande, in what is now ex-
treme western Texas. The settlements of San Lorenzo, San
Pedro de Alcántara, and Santísimo Sacramento were established at various localities twelve leagues below the Mission
of Guadalupe, now Ciudad Juárez, Mexico, as a temporary
base of operations for a return expedition into New Mexico.
This latter, in 1681, proved a failure, and Governor Otermín
decided to make San Lorenzo a more permanent settlement.
Named in honor of St. Lawrence Martyr, on whose feast-day
the Pueblo Indians had massacred twenty-one Franciscans
and several Spanish families, San Lorenzo was designated
as the Spanish town of this general region in 1681, while
the friendly Indians who chose exile with the Spaniards were assigned to three villages which were named
Senecú, Socorro, and Ysleta. Two years later, Governor
Cruzate and Father Nicolás López rearranged the colonists
by assigning the Spaniards to San Lorenzo, San Pedro,
Ysleta, and San José, and the Indians to Socorro, San Francisco, Sacramento, Senecú, and La Soledad. The following
year, in the spring of 1684, a serious uprising of the Mansos
and other wild west Texas tribes against the settlements was
put down after much bitter and heroic fighting. Even as far
back as January, 1682, the Apaches had begun raiding the
refugees, and between 1680 and 1684 other Indians of the
region had made at least five attempts to destroy the Spaniards. In the latter year, therefore, most of the Spanish
settlers were herded into San Lorenzo, headquarters of the
civil officials. So discouraged were the people by this un-
settled and precarious state of affairs that they began
petitioning for a permanent return to the safety of New
Spain. In this latter course of action they were opposed by

4

Oldest page of the Conquistadora fragments,
dated February 26, 1685

the Governor and the Franciscan Fathers.[4] Nine years later, at the close of 1693, they returned to their old Kingdom of New Mexico as *Reconquistadores*.

It was in this *Real* of San Lorenzo, and at this very period, that there existed a popular religious society or confraternity, called *La Cofradía de Nuestra Señora del Rosario La Conquistadora*. Its activities colored New Mexico life and history for many generations before and after, yet its existence is but faintly hinted at in civil and church records. Some loose sheets from the Confraternity's Inventory and Account books, fragments that lay completely forgotten for almost two centuries, however, have enabled us to reconstruct a phase of living among the people of New Mexico other than those concerning Church and State squabbles and military campaigns. The fragments are much too few in number, unfortunately, but in clearness and directness of information they leave nothing to be desired.[5]

On the very first page of the Inventory fragment is a statement by Captain Alonso del Río, *mayordomo* of the *Cofradía de Nuestra Señora La Conquistadora*, that he has received all the Confraternity's property from Francisco Gómez Robledo, who had been *mayordomo* in the preceding year of 1684. The Confraternity is in arrears because of hard times that year, as we learn from a contemporary loose

4. Anne E. Hughes, "The Beginnings of Spanish Settlement in the El Paso District." (*University of California Publications in History*, Vol. 1, No. 3), pp. 315-392. I have depended on this study for the above précis on the New Mexico exiles from 1680 to 1684.

5. Archives of the Archdiocese of Santa Fe (hereafter referred to as AASF), *Spanish Period*, No. 1. These fragments consist of a small section from an inventory book and several single sheets from different account books, all of which are designated as follows: (a) Inventory, 9 ff. (3 to 11), Feb. 26, 1685-May 1, 1704; (b) Accounts, 1 f., May 8, 1685-Feb. 2, 1689; (c) Accounts, "*Cuaderno Segundo*," 1 f., June 14, 1689; (d) Accounts, 4 ff. (1 to 4), 1713-1719; (e) Minutes, 1 f., 1717-1718; (f) Accounts, 2 ff. (63 and 97), 1717, 1724-1726. In the spring of 1947 I found these fragments in different packages labeled as miscellaneous papers, and mixed in with sundry old and modern documents. They are together now in the individual folder described above.

The historical section of the Archdiocesan Archives was begun sometime after 1935 when Archbishop Gerken had a fire-proof vault built to house all church records, which he ordered collected from parishes and missions. At this time a general assortment and filing was made. The baptismal, marriage, and burial volumes were dated and tagged, and a general classification was made of loose papers. I am deeply grateful to his Excellency, the Most Rev. Edwin V. Byrne, D.D., present Archbishop of Santa Fe, for graciously allowing me to examine this material in my search for *Franciscana* and thus, as I go along, to classify and file these treasures for historians in the future.

sheet of an Account book. We also know from history that the Mansos uprising that year had placed the settlers in dire need. Father Francisco de Vargas, in charge of San Lorenzo in 1685, signs the record together with the outgoing and incoming *mayordomos* and three deputies. The reverse side of the first Inventory sheet begins with an official Visitation by Fr. Pedro Gómez, Vice-Custos and Ecclesiastical Judge, on October 18, 1686; he finds some articles old and outworn and regulates the disposal of them; then, in his own handwriting, he makes a complete inventory of the images, clothing, jewels, and other properties, which runs through almost three pages of fine writing. The succeeding pages up to the year 1704 are filled with additional gifts by individual devotees, with *Visitas* by the various *Padres Custodios*, and with the receipts of Confraternity books and property by incoming *mayordomos*. The other loose sheets, from different account books, touching scattered years from 1685 to 1726, are filled mostly with the annual dues and names of members.

Just as no specific mention is made in contemporary outside sources of the existence of this Confraternity and its many activities, so we find no outright reference here to the political, economic, and military struggles which were going on continually. Here there is but one purpose, to honor with zealous affection "the Queen of the Angels," *Nuestra Señora del Rosario La Conquistadora.* No other mundane thing is mentioned here, except the material offerings necessary to keep her Serene Highness in a state befitting her majesty, to observe her feasts as solemnly as might be possible, and to assure the prayers and suffrages in her name for the living and deceased members of her society. Individuals who appear blazoned with glory in the annals of the Reconquest and after here appear as vassals, in the company of lesser names, at the feet of their common Queen. In short, just as the civil and military, even the ecclesiastical records of the period, give no hint of the existence of this Confraternity and its internal life, likewise a careful perusal of its few records extant provides no idea of the important historical

happenings of its times. Both, however, complement each
other, and one comes to know the early European inhabitants
of New Mexico better, singly as well as in the mass, because
of these documents.[6]

In 1691 a new and altogether different kind of Governor and Captain-General was sent to the discouraged exiles
at el Paso del Norte. Don Diego de Vargas Zapata Luján
Ponce de León was worthy of his ponderous name as a
Spanish grandee, both because of his forthright, winning
personality and the enthusiasm he instilled in most for a sure
and glorious reconquest of their northern homeland from
which they had been forcibly expelled and the re-establish-
ment of the Indian Missions. He was, moreover, a deeply
religious man. True, as others have pointed out, he had sown
his portion of wild oats in his younger days, but now in more
mature years he undertook his great task with a religious
sincerity of purpose which was never contradicted, but
rather enhanced, by his actions during his two terms as
Governor. His childlike devotion to the Virgin lights up
many a page of his *Campaign Journals* during and between
the two *Entradas* or Conquests of 1692 and 1693.

In the first purely military entry, when he received the
peaceful submission of all the Pueblos, his troops followed
a particular royal standard or banner on which was a painting of *Nuestra Señora de los Remedios,* one of the many
titles under which New World Spaniards honored Mary. De
Vargas himself seemed to be especially attached to this
name and picture. He grew almost lyrical in making the
different Pueblos submit to Her on the Standard, to whom
he continually refers as "Mary—the Virgin—Our Lady—the
Pilgrim Lady," but most often as *"Nuestra Señora de los
Remedios."*[7] His glowing reports to the Viceroy on the first
Reconquest set off extraordinary religious and civic rejoic-

6. For the sake of order and clarity, the full text of these *Conquistadora* fragments in English is appended as the closing section of this study, together with
notes connecting various items and names with historical events and persons. As a
social as well as a historical study, these facts are certainly most pertinent.

7. This title cannot be rendered properly into English. *Remedios* does mean
"remedies" or "cures." Some have translated it variously as "Our Lady of Remedies"
or "of Help" or "of Ransom." The Spanish meaning as used here connotes all these
ideas in one word.

ings in Mexico and other cities of New Spain. They also inspired the famous *Mercurio Volante*,[8] which so charmingly exaggerates de Vargas' speech regarding his Lady to the chiefs of one of the Moqui (Hopi) Pueblos.

In his second *Entrada*, the Reconquest of 1693, when he took along the seventy families of settlers with their household goods, de Vargas no longer wrote of Our Lady of *los Remedios*, but of Our Lady of the Conquest—*Nuestra Señora de la Conquista*. However, since he made no mention of any Confraternity, or the specific title of *Nuestra Señora del Rosario La Conquistadora*, his frequent use of this term was taken to mean, and not without reason, the royal standard which was triumphantly carried ahead of the troops in both *Entradas*.[9] One single reference in secular documents, which proves nothing alone, points to the Confraternity's existence: On June 17, 1692, de Vargas sent certain *Autos* of Possession of the el Paso Missions to the Viceroy, and in the accompanying letter he mentions having attended one evening the Novena and Rosary services of Our Lady of the Conquest.[10]

But neither do the Confraternity fragments make any reference to the first entry of 1692, so enthusiastically celebrated in the cities of New Spain, nor even to the second entry of 1693 with its famous battle for Santa Fe, although the pages extant cover that period. And yet, they contain some revealing passages concerning the great Reconquistador. Besides donating certain costly items to this Confraternity, de Vargas was elected, or very likely had himself elected, the *mayordomo* or President of the Confraternity from the year 1692 on. His predecessors as *mayordomos* had been ordinary minor leaders, elected more or less annually.[11]

---

8. Don Carlos Sigüenza y Góngora, *Mercurio Volante* (Los Angeles, The Quivira Society, 1932), p. 123.

9. See Note 3, "The Virgin of the Reconquest."

10. Archives of New Mexico, A. G. N., *Historia*, 37, part 3, ff. 340-341. *"y haviendo la concurrenzia de estar de novena en esta Santa Yglesia Nra. Señora de la Conquista por la tarde fui al Rosario. . . ."*

11. Inventory, f. 7. These men served as *mayordomos* in those days: Francisco Gómez Robledo (1684), Alonso del Río (1685-1691), Francisco de Anaya Almazán (1691), Cristóbal de Tapia (1692) ; during de Vargas' first term, from 1692 to 1696, the *teniente mayordomos* acting in his name were Luis Granillo (1692-1695) and Antonio Montoya (1696). De Vargas seems to have established a precedent, for later

The period following the Reconquest up to the close of the century was hectic, years of reconstruction and re-settlement amid new Indian uprisings and campaigns against the nomadic tribes. But the Confraternity's activities continued apace, except for one omission which is pointed out by the Custos, Fr. Antonio Guerra, in his *Auto de Visita*, Santa Fe, May 30, 1702. For nine years, he says (that is, since 1693), the dues-accounts had not been kept up, and so the books were full of confusion.[12] The fragments of Account books that follow, sketchily covering the period from 1713 to 1726, are very likely the results of his orders regarding a scrupulous keeping and auditing of accounts in the future. As remarked before, many outstanding things happened during this period which find no mention in these records. De Vargas was unjustly imprisoned for three years by his successor as Governor, who apparently succeeded him also as *mayordomo* of this Confraternity; he finally returned to New Spain to lay his case before the Viceroy, to come back triumphantly as a Marquis for a second term as Governor, and also as *mayordomo* of *La Conquistadora*, until his somewhat sudden death in April of 1704. Other governors came and went, and a large new parish church, the Parroquia, was a-building during the first two decades of the new century. But none of this is mentioned in the Confraternity books, just as the Confraternity is not mentioned in other documents, either secular or ecclesiastical. Yet it was fully alive and active up to the year 1726.

After 1726, for about four decades, we have no more knowledge of it, simply because not a fragment of later books of the Confraternity, if there ever were any, has yet turned up. However, some books did exist as late as 1782 when the then Custos, Fr. Juan Bermejo, started a new volume "because the old books were altogether unserviceable, which were filed where they belong."[13] Of these latter there

---

Governors appear as *mayordomos*, as noted later on. Gómez Robledo had been *mayordomo* already in 1656-9 and 1664. See note 23.

12. Inventory, f. 9, both sides.

13. AASF, Book LXXX, *Libro donde se asientan los Cofrades de Ntra. Sra. del Rosario*, ff. 1-2. This leather-bound volume consists of forty-six *fojas;* up to f. 31 the pages are filled with the names of Santa Fe and *vecino* members, December 31,

is now no trace. Moreover, we know that a Confraternity did exist twelve years prior to Fr. Bermejo's new book of 1782 from two other still old sources which are graphically distinct and different in treating the same subject. These are the famous *Report* of Fr. Atanasio Domínguez and the *Noticias* of Juan Candelaria, both written in the same year, 1777.[14] On an official Visitation to the Franciscan Missions of New Mexico, Fr. Domínguez described with discerning eye all the good and the bad that he found in the friars' administration of the Missions and the state of their churches and convents, with particular emphasis on the *Villa* of Santa Fe. Regarding church societies, Fr. Domínguez enthusiastically approved of the *Cofradía de Nuestra Señora de la Luz* which had been established seventeen years before in the military chapel of Our Lady of Light, the *Castrense*. Not only was this relatively new chapel a marvel to behold among the poorer and more antique Missions, but its sodality's papers of canonical foundation were in good order. Not so, however, the *Cofradía de Nuestra Señora del Rosario*, which looked like a spurious thing to him. Listen how he tells it:

> There is no canonically chosen Patron Saint in this Kingdom of New Mexico, as there is in most parts of Kingdoms, Provinces, Cities, Villas, etc., and although among the common people Our Lady of the Rosary is said to be it, this is not so: and this vulgar opinion takes its origin from what has happened in the years from 1770 to the present one of 77. . . .[15]

"What has happened in the years from 1770 to the present one of 77" is revealed by the Candelaria account. Unlike the most efficient and well-lettered Friar-Visitator from Mexico City, old Juan Candelaria wrote simply but with

1819. The rest of the book, mostly blank, contains a few scattered entries, most of them written in a very poor hand, without system and dates. Two exceptions are the more or less orderly entries for 1845 and 1848, the result of Bishop Zubiría's visit.

14. Fray Atanasio Domínguez, *Report*. N. M. Arch., *Bibl. Nac. de Mex.*, 10, part 2, ff. 4115 *et. seq.; "Noticias* of Juan Candelaria," NEW MEXICO HISTORICAL REVIEW, IV, 274-297. These reminiscences were written in 1776-1777 by an old resident of Albuquerque who claimed to have been born in 1692. The original or a copy of it found its way to Mexico long ago, and a transcript of it was given to Dr. Sylvanus G. Morley by Don Federico Gómez de Orozco of Mexico City.

15. *Op. cit.*, f. 4115. "No ai en este *Reyno de Nuevo-Mex.co S.o Patron jurado, como lo ai en las mas partes de Reynos, Provincias, Ciudades, Villas, etc, y aunque vulgarmente se dice serlo N. S. del Rosario, no es assi: y esta vulgaridad toma su origen por lo sucedido en los años desde 1770 hasta el presente de 77. . . ."

Libro donde se asientan los Cofrades de Ntra. Sra. del Rosario que con aprovacion del Sor. R. P. Cust Vicario y Juez eclesiast. R. P. Mntro y Diputad. de la indicada Cofradia formo el Mayordomo Vizte. Froncoso atento á lo incervible que estan los antiguos Libros. Constando este de Ciento quarenta y seis fojas. Abril 21 de 1782.

Title page of the membership and dues book of the Rosario Confraternity in its second phase. It is dated April 21, 1782

patriotic pride, covering the same points and period as Fr. Domínguez in this matter. After giving a very faulty "traditional" history of New Mexico up to his day, this old native ended his "Accounts" with a contemporary event which was fresh in his memory. In the year 1770, he wrote, the people of the Kingdom were in dire straits from the continuous attacks made against them by their "barbarian enemies," the wild Apaches, Comanches, and Navajos. And because there was no other recourse left but to turn to God, the people decided to elect a special heavenly Patron to intercede for them before the Divine Majesty:

> Well aware of the fact that the most powerful intercession before the Omnipotent is His most holy Mother, whose Holy Image, with the title *del Rosario*, is venerated in the Parish Church of this Villa of Santa Fe, brought there by the Conquistador Don Diego de Vargas, for which cause they call her *La Conquistadora*, the inhabitants resolved to elect her as specially sworn Patroness of said Kingdom, and that a yearly church-function be celebrated in her honor in said Church, with the greatest solemnity possible, on the first Sunday of October.[16]

Candelaria goes on to tell how the *vecinos* applied to Governor Mendinueta, who referred them to the Franciscans so that they might publish the proposal in all the Missions. This was done, and from this time was born a Confraternity with its annually elected *mayordomos*, its dues in kind collected from all over the Kingdom, and its special festival on the first Sunday of October. The first *mayordomos* in 1771 were Don Carlos and Don Bartolomé Fernández; in 1772, Don Antonio José Ortiz and Don Blas García; in 1773, Don Francisco Trébol Navarro and Don Diego Antonio Baca; in 1774, Don Toribio Ortiz and Don Manuel Sáenz de Garviso; in 1775, Don Juan Antonio Ortiz and Don José Galves; and in 1776, Don Antonio José Ortiz, for a second term, who offered himself as perpetual *mayordomo* with the help of Don Cristóbal Vigil.

> This Festivity continues without fail until the present year of 77 . . . and it is hoped that it will be perpetuated because of the palpable favors which, through the powerful intercession of the

---

16. *Op. cit.*, pp. 293-295.

Sovereign Queen of all things created, have been experienced and are being experienced.

Thus end the *Noticias* of Juan Candelaria. According to both him and Fr. Domínguez, the choice of Our Lady of the Rosary, *La Conquistadora*, as special patroness of New Mexico, and the institution of her Confraternity with its festivals, were something altogether new, the result of a popular movement which took place seven years previously. The inescapable conclusion from these two accounts so dissimilar, yet so complementary, is that by 1770 the old Confraternity of *La Conquistadora* had been completely forgotten. The *antiguos libros inservibles* mentioned by Fr. Bermejo in 1782 were merely the accounts and minutes that had been kept since 1770, for in his 1776 tour of New Mexico, after which he wrote his critique, Fr. Domínguez complained of the Confraternity's not being of canonical establishment and of the people's recent unauthorized election of Our Lady of the Rosary, *La Conquistadora* (to him a vulgar title), as sworn Patroness of New Mexico. He apparently knew nothing, nor did the local friars themselves know anything, of these few earlier fragments that have turned up in our time. These, as one may judge from their excellent condition, must have lain pressed and hidden from destructive sunlight and other elements in some old leather-bound baptismal or marriage volume, or among undisturbed sheaves of matrimonial investigations. These loose sheets seem to have been taken out only in recent years, only to be consigned, unnoticed, to packages of "miscellaneous papers."[17]

How long the Confraternity lasted in its first phase after 1726, it is impossible to say. Perhaps it dwindled gradually through the next thirty-four years, to die a natural death. Perhaps it received the final *coup de grace* while in its dying condition from the establishment of a new and rival society having similar aims and procedure. This is why the Confraternity of Our Lady of Light deserves special attention here. The new Marian society was inaugurated

---

17. See Note 5.

with great fanfare in 1760-1761 by the then Governor, Don Francisco Marín del Valle, in connection with the erection of the new military chapel of the same title, with its now famous stone reredos.[18] The Governor even had its Constitutions printed in Mexico City, and Bishop Tamarón of Durango, in Santa Fe on one of those very rare episcopal Visitations to New Mexico, had been present at its very first meeting.

Some writers have advanced the idea that Governor del Valle, because he was partial to the Jesuits and disliked the friars, sought to replace the Franciscans in New Mexico with them. That he did favor the Society of Jesus was nothing untoward, for individuals in the Church have at all times favored this or that Order or Society as a result of family or educational connections, or some other factor. To say that this Governor was hostile to the Franciscans as such is not quite correct. True, the Confraternity of Our Lady of Light had been introduced into New Spain by the Jesuits, and Marín del Valle did include a representation of the Jesuits' Founder, St. Ignatius Loyola, in one of the reredos' main panels, also dedicating one of the side-altars to that great Jesuit missionary, St. Francis Xavier. But on an equal footing with St. Ignatius of Loyola, in a companion-panel, he placed St. Francis Solano, the Franciscan Apostle of South America; and on the frontal of the *mensa*, or front center-panel of the altar-table, was a stone carving of the Franciscan St. Anthony of Padua. In the inaugural festivities which were spread over five days, the Franciscan friars played important parts. At the solemn blessing of the chapel by the secular Vicar in the afternoon of May 23, 1761, the Franciscan Custos, Fr. Jacobo de Castro, and seven other friars were present; on the following day Fr. de Castro preached at the Mass celebrated by the Vicar, Don Santiago Roybal; on the twenty-fifth he himself was the celebrant and Fr. Miguel Campos preached; on the twenty-sixth Fr.

---

18. A. von Wuthenau, "The Spanish Military Chapels in Santa Fé and Reredos of Our Lady of Light," NEW MEXICO HISTORICAL REVIEW, X, 175-194; Eleanor B. Adams, "The Chapel and Cofradía of Our Lady of Light in Santa Fe," *Ibid.*, XXII, 327-341.

Manuel Rojo from Albuquerque had the Mass and the sermon was delivered by Fr. Francisco Guzmán; on the twenty-seventh Fr. Joaquín Pérez sang a Requiem Mass for the deceased members.[19] Probably the first military chaplain appointed to the *Castrense* was Fr. Juan Bermejo, who was serving in this capacity when the first *Castrense* marriage-book was begun in 1779; he served until the spring of 1787, and was succeeded by Fr. Francisco de Hozio, who kept this post until his death, September 24, 1823.[20] What is more, Fr. Atanasio Domínguez was most enthusiastic about the new Confraternity in his Visitation of 1776, whereas he expressed some dislike for the more ancient and venerable one of *La Conquistadora*. All this serves to show that the latter was not killed off by any "Jesuitic leanings" on the part of the Governor or the secular Vicar General, if indeed the Confraternity of *La Conquistadora* still existed as late as 1760. On the contrary, the local friars themselves had allowed it to languish sometime between 1726 and 1760, and the vigorous and colorful new society perhaps dealt it the final death blow. At any rate, the *Conquistadora* Confraternity was not only dead, but forgotten as well, when the inhabitants of 1770, in order to be delivered from the Apache scourge of that day, re-chose the same Lady of the Rosary, their *La Conquistadora*, as Patroness of the Kingdom, and inaugurated a Confraternity with a special festival, as they must have supposed, for the first time.

This totally new *Conquistadora* Confraternity showed great vitality for the next few decades, at least up to the year 1819. The gloriously inaugurated Lady of Light Confraternity seems to have petered out a few years after Domínguez Visit and Report, or at least was confined to the garrison families attached to the *Castrense* chapel. Then, too, a new Confraternity "of the Blessed Sacrament" had been founded in the latter half of the eighteenth century which, as early as 1774, had merged with that of the Rosary.

---

19. *Ibid.*, pp. 328-333. A compressed account in English of Fr. Domínguez' account. It is to this Franciscan's enthusiasm that we owe most of our knowledge of Our Lady of Light.
20. AASF, Marriage-51 and Burial-51, *Castrense;* Burial-52, *Santa Fé.*

At that period and after, the *mayordomos* and the majority of members of both Societies seem to have been the same.[21] After 1819, the movement dwindled, so far as account book entries show.

To sum up, it is now an established fact that a Confraternity under the specific title of *Nuestra Señora del Rosario La Conquistadora* existed among the people of New Mexico at the *Real* of San Lorenzo four years after the Indian Revolt of 1680 and nine years prior to the Reconquest in 1693. It was still full of life in New Mexico in 1726, but seems to have been altogether forgotten by 1770, so that its second phase, begun in the latter year, turned out to be not so much a revival of the old as an altogether new Confraternity, but, according to Fr. Domínguez, not canonically established. This latter Confraternity, merged by 1774 with that of the Blessed Sacrament, continued in force until 1819, then sporadically until the era of the American Occupation, and was apparently altogether extinct when the American Diocese of Santa Fe was founded in 1850.

The problem that remains to be solved is that of antiquity. How long before 1684, our earliest specific date in these fragments, did the Confraternity exist as such? Certainly it existed in New Mexico before the Revolt of 1680 and the flight south of the Spanish refugees to the el Paso district and their founding of San Lorenzo. Besides Fr. Gómez' condemnation of certain properties of the Confraternity as outworn by 1686, there is one specific reference to its still earlier existence: Prior to May, 1693, an entry was

---

21. Two civil documents of that year show this merger. On June 16, 1774, a Manuel de Arteaga, *"mayordomo de las Cofradías de Nuestro Amo, y de Nuestra Señora del Rosario,"* made a complaint before Governor Mendinueta against his predecessor, Don Tomás de Sena, concerning the number of sheep belonging to the Confraternities. Then, on July 13, 1774, Sena himself presented the same complaint against Alonso García, who took care of the flocks *"del dibiníssimo y de Ntra Señora del Rosario,"* even at the time of a former *mayordomo*, Sena's deceased father. R. E. Twitchell, *Spanish Archives of New Mexico*, II, nos. 677 and 679.—Also, AASF, Book LXXX, *Cofrades de Ntra. Sra. del Rosario*, f. 22. Identical in format and leather binding is Book LXXIX, *Cofrades de Nuestro Amo y Sor Sacramentado*, ordered concurrently with the former by Fr. Bermejo in 1782. The title-page is all the same, except for the Confraternity name, and Don Vicente Troncoso appears as *mayordomo* of either society; likewise, the first list of members in either volume is headed by Governor de Anza and his wife. See also *Sp. Arch.*, II, no. 1360, *"Ynventario de la Alajas, etc.,* and no. 1993, Fr. Pereyro's Report in 1808.

made at San Lorenzo concerning "a silver lamp which was brought out of New Mexico which was kept at the Convent of Socorro [Texas] and was returned to the Confraternity because it was its property."[22]

A much older and most important reference to a Confraternity of the same name, which we have every reason to believe is the same one, is the casual mention of it by Francisco Gómez Robledo in his defense before the Inquisition in Mexico City, February 13, 1664.[23] Gómez Robledo declared that he had heard Fray Miguel Sacristán, Guardian in Santa Fe during Governor Manso's term (1656-1659), say something pertinent to the case when he went to the Father's cell to take some clothing belonging to the Confraternity of Our Lady of the Rosary, because he (Gómez Robledo) was its *Mayordomo* at the time, as he was also now at the time of his trial. This same man was *Mayordomo* again in 1684.

A very significant reference, kindly furnished by Dean Scholes of the Graduate School of the University of New Mexico, may indeed push the date of the Confraternity still further back. On April 11, 1626, Fray Pedro Zambrano, Guardian of Galisteo, declared that the impious Governor Eulate (1618-1625) had ordered a certain Juan de Olvera falsely accused and hanged because he was a pious man "and deputy of the Confraternity of the Mother of God *de la Concepción*."[23a]

The "old books," ordered preserved by Fr. de Vargas in 1691, and then ordered destroyed by Fr. Hinojosa in 1692,[24] might have dated back to Governor Manso's time and even earlier.

A consideration of the unusual title, *La Conquistadora*, also provides material for speculation. It is a unique name, a popular and not an ecclesiastical title of Mary which was

22. Inventory, f. 7.
23. A. G. N., *Inquisición*, 583, f. 370. *"Y que este confesante oyo decir a Fray Miguel Sacristan . . . siendo Guardian de la Villa de Santa Fee, en tiempo que era Gobernador Don Juan Manso, Yendo este a su celda a llevarle ropa perteneciente a la Cofradía de nuestra Señora del Rosario por que este era su Mayordomo y de presente lo era."*
23a. A. G. N., *Inquisición*, t. 356, f. 278v.
24. *Ibid.*, f. 6, both sides.

added to the sanctioned appellation of Our Lady of the
Rosary. This latter has a long tradition, based on the
"Rosary," which comes from the pre-medieval practice of
saying the Lord's Prayer and the Ave Maria a certain number of times while a person contemplates different phases of
the Savior's life; actual count was kept of these prayers
on a string with knots or beads. (In fact, our English word
"bead" derives from these strings of knots or balls from the
old Anglo-Saxon word, "to pray.") Poetry came in early and
called these strings, and the prayers said with them, the
"rosarius," meaning a garland or crown of roses. In the
thirteenth century, St. Dominic of Gusmán, a famous
Spanish preacher and canon who founded the Dominican
Order at the same time that St. Francis of Assisi founded
the Franciscan Order, popularized this praying of the Rosary. Through his first disciples this practice more or less took
its present form. By the fifteenth century, Confraternities of
the Holy Rosary were widespread not only in southern
Europe but also in Germany and England as well. The
Blessed Virgin Mary acquired a new title, and this became
famous on the first Sunday of October, 1571, the day the
Confraternity in Rome prayed the Rosary in procession
through the streets while the Christians under Don Juan of
Austria fought the famed naval battle of Lepanto, a decisive
victory over the Saracens, who had threatened to overrun
Europe. Pope St. Pius V, himself a Dominican friar, ordered a solemn commemoration of the Rosary to be made
yearly on this day.

The above digression has a deep bearing on our problem. Here we have a seventeenth-century Spanish colony
with an active Confraternity of the Holy Rosary, which
was a devotion popularized by Dominic the Spaniard, a
name and title made glorious by the victory over the Saracens by a Spanish fleet in one of the greatest naval engage-
ments of all time. Moreover, the Franciscans were in charge
of the New Mexico Missions, and a close traditional tie
existed, and has come down to our day, between these two
sister-Orders from the time Francis and Dominic met in
Rome while seeking Papal approval of their respective foun-

dations. Lepanto was only some eighty years way from the decade before 1656, near the time when the Confraternity may have been founded in New Mexico. Could it be that these people called their own Lady of the Rosary a "Lady-Conqueror" in memory of Lepanto? Or did the name arise in that year of 1684 when the refugees at San Lorenzo, placing themselves under her protection, put down the dangerous Mansos insurrection? Or, indeed, does the name hark back to the days of Cortés and his Conquest of Mexico?[25] Or did the New Mexicans call her *Conquistadora* because she had come to New Mexico between the years 1598 and 1650 with their own parents and grandparents, to whom they always referred with pride as *conquistadores* of the Kingdom? This point will be developed further when we treat of the statue itself. While it does not help us in establishing definitely the Confraternity's date of origin, it most certainly is a unique title, and a local one as well.[26]

---

25. See Note 5, references to Cortés legend.
26. Many have rendered the name into English as "Our Lady of Victory." This is a wrong translation because "Our Lady of Victory" is a distinct, sanctioned title with its own shrine and history. This mistranslation originated after 1851 with the French clergy who, from the similarity in concept between "conquest" and "victory" and from their acquaintance with the famous shrine and confraternity of *Notre Dame des Victoires* in Paris, started the use of the erroneous title, *Nuestra Señora de la Victoria*, among the native people themselves. DeFouri and Salpointe are the first to use this title in print, in preference to the correct traditional names.

CHAPTER II

THE CONQUISTADORA STATUE

A religious society of the sort of which we have been treating revolved about a specific image of the society's Patron Saint, whether the latter be a painting on canvas or any flat surface, a bas-relief on wood or yeso, or a statue in the round of any material whatsoever. The material representation of the Rosary Confraternity's Patroness is described, fortunately, in the earlier *Conquistadora* document extant when Fr. Pedro Gómez wrote out a three-page inventory on October 18, 1686. The inventory begins with "First of all, the figure of *Nuestra Señora La Conquistadora*, of a *vara* in height, a little more, in the round."[27] Next follows a list of her dresses, mantles, jewels, and other images and valuables of her Confraternity. The next direct mention of the statue occurs on February 3, 1697, when Captain Alonso Rael de Aguilar takes over as Assistant *Mayordomo* of her Confraternity in the Governor's name and receives "First of all, *Nuestra Señora La Conquistadora* with dress and mantle, silver crown, and an Agnus-Dei and a reliquary and a Rosary."[28] These are the only direct references, prior to 1777, to this image as a statue in the round and not a painting, although the lists of her dresses and the frequent donations of more dresses and crowns leave no room for doubt as to the fact that these articles belonged to a statue in the round.

The 1777 descriptions are interesting. Despite his prejudices regarding the Confraternity, Father Domínguez was quite taken by the statue:

> In the large niche there is an image in the round of Our Lady of the Rosary (or as others say, of *La Conquistadora*), of a *vara* in height, and although already old it is newly retouched. It has many and good ornaments; but since it is always getting a complete change, its current dress is not described now; yes, it only wears continually

27. "*Primeramente la echura de Nra. Sra. La conquistadora, de bara de alto poco mas, de bulto—*" Inventory, f. 3v. A *vara* was 32.99 inches.
28. "*Primeramente nuestra Señora La conquistadora con bestido y ornamento corona de Plata y Un agnus y Un biril y Rozario.*" *Ibid.*, f. 8

[without being changed] a wig, a little tortoise-shell *bâton* wound around with solid silver threads, and dabbed with the same, with the knob gilded, and a silver half-moon at its feet over the dress.[29]

Later on, Father Domínguez lists her clothing and mentions three chests in the sacristy of her chapel for keeping them. Juan Candelaria merely states that it was a "Sacred Image," but he also says that Governor Mendinueta paid for "a dress for the Image, of the best silk he found in Mexico, and a chest with key in which it is kept. . . ."[30]

This matter of identifying the statue as such must be emphasized, because, prior to the discovery of the *Conquistadora* fragments, historians identified "Our Lady of the Conquest" mentioned by de Vargas with the royal banner of "Our Lady of *los Remedios*." Consequently, there was considerable doubt that the famous statue of Our Lady of the Rosary, popularly called *La Conquistadora*, and treasured from time immemorial in the Santa Fe Parroquia, dated from the Reconquest period as popular tradition insisted. Because of its continual presence in the Parroquia, and the tradition of its being brought to Santa Fe when the *Villa* was wrested from the Indians, the old inhabitants held that this very image was the same one which de Vargas had brought with him. So deeply rooted was this belief, indeed, that, even after the de Vargas *Journals* in the Palace of the Governors were more carefully examined many decades ago, no incongruity was noticed between the statue which they had and the patent description of the standard of Our Lady which is mentioned so often in the *Journals*. Perhaps the people may have thought the statue could have been lashed in some way to an unright pennant-type standard, an idea which I myself entertained as logical and possible before a thorough study of the *Journals* brought out the improbability of such a practice. The more serious pioneers in local historical research, like Mr. Twitchell and Mr. Read, seem to have left this delicate question of the statue alone, out of respect for such a beautiful popular tradition if not from fear of incurring popular anger, while Mr. Prince, although

---

29. *Op. cit.*, ff. 4128-4129.
30. *Op. cit.*, p. 295.

unable to accept Father DeFouri's arguments to support the tradition, was as sympathetic as any honest historian can be. At the time these good men wrote there was no knowledge of the 1777 Domínguez *Report* nor of the Candelaria *Noticias*, and even these would have left them eighty-four years later than 1693 without any earlier documentary proof. For an enthusiast, there was no need of further documentary witnesses. If the people had always believed that this very statue, which is several centuries old beyond all doubt, was the one which came with de Vargas, and two documents written in 1777 testified that in 1770 there was a statue of Our Lady of the Rosary venerated in the Santa Fe Parroquia (and called *La Conquistadora* because it was brought thither by de Vargas), then the seventy-seven-year span between that year and the year of the Reconquest was nothing compared with the seventy-seven plus one hundred years during which the tradition was kept alive from 1770 to 1947.

These newly-discovered sources, however, bridge the gap. What is more, they clarify some disputed and seemingly contradictory passages in the de Vargas *Journals*. It was with these statements of de Vargas in mind that Dr. Espinosa essayed a plausible solution of the Santa Fe tradition and was forced to conclude by the evidence then at hand "that the present image of *La Conquistadora* is not the original one brought by Governor Vargas in 1693, or else that it was converted into a Virgen del Rosario sometime after reconquest days." Our present knowledge of the existence of both the Confraternity and the statue prior to the period of the Reconquest, and even of the Revolt of 1680, enables us to elucidate de Vargas' meaning in several telling passages. There is no doubt at all that in the first entry of 1692, he referred his successes to the Virgin in her title of *los Remedios* as represented on the royal standard. But, like any well-informed Catholic, he really loved and venerated Mary in her person in Heaven; although so closely attached to this particular title that at the hour of death he specifically remembered it,[31] he saw the same person in other titles and

---

31. *Sp. Arch.*, I, No. 1027. In the codicil to his will, Bernalillo, April 9, 1704, he commends his soul, through Masses to be said in her honor, to "*Nuestra Señora de*

images as well. For instance, on his return from Puebloland to his headquarters at el Paso del Norte, he thanked Mary under a different title entirely for his peaceful conquest of 1692: "I entered the holy temple, the church of Our Lady of Guadalupe, to give thanks to her blessed Majesty for my happy arrival and the victory gained through her most holy will and intercession."[32]

Hence, months before the second entry, in which all the colonists were to take part in order to resettle the land, de Vargas readily became acquainted with the original New Mexicans' particular devotion to Mary and quickly identified himself with the aspirations of his subjects as embodied in their favorite image of his own beloved Queen. In 1692 he was elected *Mayordomo* of her Confraternity, on which occasion he donated a complete set of damask vestments and other valuable articles; and he kept the presidency of the society all during his term as Governor and Captain-General of New Mexico.[33] From this we know what he meant, and to whom he referred, when he wrote to the Viceroy from el Paso del Norte on January 12, 1693:

> It is my wish, and of those with whom I enter, including the soldiers, that they should, first and foremost, personally build the church and holy temple, setting up in it before all else the patroness of the said Kingdom and *Villa*, who is the one that was saved from the fury of the savages, her title being Our Lady of the Conquest. And so, with the aid of the soldiers and settlers, the foundations will be laid and the walls of the holy temple raised. . . .[34]

From the native exiles of New Mexico—the settlers, the soldiers, and the captains, who had fought their way out of Santa Fe in 1680—the new Governor learned about the "Patroness" of the Kingdom of New Mexico and its capital, the very one "that was saved from the fury of the savages."

los Remedios, my protectress." The inventory of his effects, April 20, 1704, mentions another image as his private possession: "*una Ymagen de Nuestra Señora de la defensa de talla de una terzia de alto con su coronita y pilar de plata que pesara dos marcos.*" *Ibid.*, II, 100, f. 6.

32. J. Manuel Espinosa, *First Expedition of Vargas into New Mexico, 1692.* (Coronado Series Vol. X, Albuquerque, 1940), p. 251. See also A. G. I., *Guadalajara,* 139.

33. Inventory, f. 8.

34. J. Manuel Espinosa, *op. cit.*, p. 284. A. G. I., *Guad.*, 139.

Someone had carried her out of Santa Fe on that memorable August day when the besieged inhabitants fled from the capital, fighting all the way south while they carried the aged and wounded and whatsoever of their prized possessions which were not too cumbersome.[35] Before coming to San Lorenzo this Virgin had had her own special *throne* in Santa Fe, and now de Vargas himself was going to have the privilege of restoring her to it, as he wrote to the Viceroy, on October 13, when starting out on the second entry:

We left for Santa Fe under the protection of Our Lady of the Conquest. . . .[36]

I have given an account to your Excellency of everything, and of bringing into the same city and placing in it its patroness and protectress, Our Lady of the Conquest, the glory and pride being mine that I shall not only be the one who shall place it in its *Villa* of Santa Fe, but also I shall place it upon a new throne and place which I shall have to rebuild for her sovereign and divine majesty.[37]

Here, and from the whole tenor of the *Journals* besides, we see that, while the *Remedios* banner again led the soldiers on the 1693 campaign, the Captain-General was all-enthusiastic about the New Mexican's own especial patroness. That he always used the term *"Nuestra Señora de la Conquista"* instead of *"La Conquistadora"* betrays his noble and refined upbringing. Only the common people would dare to be so familiar with the Celestial Queen, like those of Mexico today who refer to *Nuestra Señora de Guadalupe* as *"La Guadalupana"* and *"La Morenita del Tepeyac."*

By December the de Vargas Expedition had reached Santo Domingo Pueblo, where a halt was called in order to rest and to replenish food supplies. Here, on December 4, the Governor had an interview with an Indian chief from the Tanos pueblos who argued that his people were restless be-

---

35. Undoubtedly other images were taken out by the refugees as, for example, the small statues and paintings owned by the Confraternity. In the early nineteenth century, a Mexican official wrote in a report to his superiors, speaking of the Pueblo Revolt, that a missionary had carried out with him "an image of the Virgin, called Our Lady of the War-Club, which is venerated in the great convent of San Francisco in Mexico." Lansing B. Bloom, "Barreiro's Ojeada Sobre Nuevo-Mexico," NEW MEXICO HISTORICAL REVIEW, III, 76.

36. J. Manuel Espinosa, "The Virgin of the Reconquest," p. 80. A. G. N., *Historia*, t. 37, Mexico.

37. *Sp. Arch.*, II, 54a, ff. 9-10.

cause of their distrust of the vengeful Spaniards. De Vargas swore complete safety for the Indians, naming as witness *"la Virgen Maria Nuestra Señora y a la Santa Cruz del Rosario."*[38] This and another quotation, treated at length in the footnote below, though far from conclusive, are given in order to present all possible references to the subject in the de Vargas Campaign *Journals.*

Finally the Expedition reached Santa Fe. The Spanish troops and the settlers set up camps outside the town walls, while their leader parleyed with the Tanos tribe that had occupied the capital since the Revolt. Then:

> On the 16th day of December, date and year above [1693], I, the said Governor and Captain-General, about the eleventh hour of the same day, made my entry into the *Villa* of Santa Fe . . . the Captain, Don Fernando Duran de Chaves, carrying the standard referred to in these acts, and under which this land was conquered, we arrived at the plaza. . . .[39]

On December 18, de Vargas made a tour of the town for a specific purpose, and, finding the parish church completely in ruins, crossed the small river to the chapel of San Miguel:

> On account of the inclemency of the weather and the urgent necessity of having a church in which might be celebrated the divine office and the Holy Sacrifice of the Mass, and in order that Our Lady of the Conquest might have a suitable place, I . . . realized that it would be expedient and proper to roof said walls . . . and being within the plaza of this village, I ordered the natives . . . to proceed with said labor cheerfully . . . to make a house for the Lord and his most

---

38. *Ibid.,* No. 54b, f. 60v, line 10, which checks with A. G. N., *Historia,* 38, f. 57, nos. 45-46. The reading is identical in both MSS. It is a strange expression, as there is no such official or popular title of "The Holy Cross of the Rosary." It could well be that he referred to the rosary itself, the amanuensis using capital letters here as indiscriminately as small ones were used elsewhere instead of capitals. However, "and of the Holy Cross" may be read parenthetically, thus connecting "of the Rosary" with "Our Lady." On December 10 there was another interview with a Captain Cristóval of San Marcos Pueblo; referring to his gestures of pardon the previous year, de Vargas argued that he could not be deceived by the devil because he had in his company "the Virgin Our Lady in that . . . Standard, which I had in my tent, and likewise I showed them *el Rosario* and the other relics and images of my devotion." *Sp. Arch.,* II, 54b, f. 33. (Very fragile and much text missing from crumbled margin.)

The word *tienda* was a military term for a field-tent, and perhaps this was the *"tienda de Campania de Lona grande con sus palos y yerros bien tratada,"* mentioned in the inventory of de Vargas' effects, April 20, 1704.—*Ibid.,* No. 100, f. 5v.

39. The banner is called *"Estandarte"* in *Sp. Arch.,* II, No. 54c, and *"Pendon"* in A. G. N., *Hist.,* 38, *Autos de Guerra,* ff. 61-64.

blessed Mother, our Virgin Lady, who was enclosed in a wagon, and that if a lady should come to any one of them, they would be obliged to furnish her with a house. . . .[40]

These two quotations are here run consecutively to suggest the separate identities of the Royal Standard and Our Lady of the Conquest. On December 16, de Vargas made his Grand Entry into the plaza, where, with customary religious and military pomp, he took possession of the *Villa* and Kingdom once more; most prominent in all this pageantry was the Standard bearing the picture of Our Lady of *los Remedios*. But two days later, de Vargas himself is looking for a suitable place for Mass, since winter was setting in fast; finding the old Parroquia completely destroyed, he proceeded to Analco, the village across the Santa Fe stream where stood the walls of the chapel of San Miguel. The Indians had burnt off the roof in 1680, but even after thirteen years the stout walls still survived. A new roof would make the church usable, at least temporarily. Here was the best place available for a church until the new Parroquia was raised, and also, of course, for a new throne, if only a temporary one, for the old Patroness of the Kingdom and *Villa*, Our Lady of the Conquest. When the Captain-General made this last knightly suggestion to the Tanos, who were not nearly so chivalrous in their regard of the female sex, they must have looked about for the Lady, whereupon de Vargas had to explain that she was still wrapped up and boxed in one of the wagons. No stretch of the imagination is needed now to distinguish between the picture on the Standard and another image of some sort. Usually the former was carried by an official *alférez* or standard-bearer, and at other times it was kept in the Governor's tent; for the last few days it had been very much in evidence, what with all these troop maneuvers and grandiose pageants. But the San Miguel chapel had to be re-roofed and renovated in order to receive another and a different representation of the Lady, and this was still enclosed in one of the wagons, probably the *carro* carrying the property of her Confratern-

---

40. A. G. N., *Hist.*, 89, ff. 67-68.

ity. Even if the fragments of its pre-Reconquest books had not been discovered, one could deduce from all this the existence of the statue returning to a former throne. Always bending backward, as the phrase goes, to please the Indians and be fair to them, de Vargas allowed the Tanos plenty of time to gather their effects and evacuate the town. Meanwhile the troops and the colonists established their camps outside the walls. But the Indians were in no hurry to leave. The weather grew bitterly cold. The weaker colonists were dying of exposure, and representatives from among them remonstrated before the Governor. In the meantime the Indians had barricaded themselves behind the walls, and on December 28 they began to taunt the Spaniards. De Vargas launched an attack the following morning, a siege of wall-storming and of counter-attacks by other Indian forces from the north, which lasted until nightfall. During this battle the Royal Standard was borne into the fray. Before daybreak of December 30, the Spaniards stormed the walls again, and dawn found them masters of the situation. Soon the Standard was flying from the highest tower of the Palace of the Governors. No mention of a statue, or even of Our Lady of the Conquest, is made in the detailed accounts of the battle. The Standard, which actually was a battle-flag, went out on other campaigns the following year.[41]

41. AASF, *Spanish Period,* no. 2, de Vargas' description of his discovery of the remains of the friar-martyr of Jemez.

What eventually became of the royal standard, nobody seems to know. Juan Páez Hurtado, in his inventory of de Vargas' effects, lists "three standards, two of them embroidered."—*Sp. Arch.,* II, No. 100, f. 5v. But shortly before that, in his will, de Vargas himself declared two banners as his personal property, "those of Anselm and St. Michael the Great," neither of which fits the description of the *Remedios* Standard. *Sp. Arch.,* I, No. 1027. Perhaps the third one, not embroidered, included by Hurtado, is the one. In the *Conquistadora* fragments themselves, a "*Nuestra Señora del Rosario en el guion*" is mentioned with other paintings.—Inventory, f. 8, February 3, 1697. And in a decree of April 26, 1707, Gov. Cuervo y Valdés ordered that due honors must be paid the royal Standard-bearer when carrying it.— *Sp. Arch.,* II, No. 843, f. 8. Since the Parroquia was not yet built, nor the San Miguel chapel restored, the Parish and Confraternity headquarters must have been in the tower-chapel of the Palace of the Governors; and since the Governors at this period were also *mayordomos* of the Confraternity, it could be that the Standard is this guidon mentioned, though misnamed.

A 1796 inventory of the Rosary Confraternity's valuables numbers among many items "*Una Señora de Los Remedios de pincel,* [*que vino?*] *con la conquista de este Reyno.*" *Ibid.,* no. 1360. Now, there is in the Cathedral Museum an old painting on

Twenty years passed, a period of material rebuilding in the capital as well as the *villas* and *estancias* up and down the Rio Grande Valley. De Vargas, after being cruelly treated by his successor, came back for a second term, but died in 1704. That his complete exploits were already beclouded in the minds of the practically letterless populace can be seen in a Governor's edict in 1712, when an annual Fiesta was proclaimed to commemorate the de Vargas bloodless Reconquest of 1692. This first entry, engraved in the memories of the inhabitants of New Spain by the public celebrations it occasioned and by the publication of the *Mercurio Volante*, had obscured his more epic entry with the settlers in 1693 and the subsequent dramatic battle for Santa Fe. The faint memory of a battle remained, however; how it fitted in with the bloodless Reconquest of 1692 was a problem to be solved in a most natural way. Since there was no bloodshed in the supposedly one and only Reconquest, therefore the battle they remembered was bloodless; since there was a Lady-Conqueror in their midst, and she had come with de Vargas, it was because of her that no blood was shed; since her name was *"La Conquistadora,"* she must have actually led the troops into battle. Thus the legend was born, erroneously confirmed more than a century later

canvas of the Virgin and Child; it is attached to the rear of a wooden rococo panel with an oval opening which once was a part of an altar-screen in the old Parroquia. I am almost sure that it represents Our Lady of *los Remedios;* what principally drew my attention to it is the fact that the canvas did not belong there originally, for it is too long for the panel, so that about six inches of the bottom is folded back; what is more, along the vertical edges on the rear of the canvas are strips of red silk suggesting the idea that it might have once been attached to a larger piece of fabric— a banner, for example.

In his *First Expedition of Vargas* . . ., Dr. Espinosa states that the *Remedios* Standard was the one brought by Oñate (p. 59, footnote), but he gives no reference. However, it does not tally with two descriptions of banners of Oñate's time: 1) the standard provided by Luis de Velasco of figured white Castilian silk stamped on one side with the picture of Our Lady and St. John the Baptist, both surrounded by a rosary and with Oñate's escutcheon at their feet; the reverse had a picture of St. James on horseback with the Velasco arms at its feet.—Twitchell, *Old Santa Fe* (Santa Fe, 1925), p. 27. 2) The banner in possession of Ensign Juan Muñoz who came to New Mexico in 1600, "a standard of red damask . . . having two emblems of Our Lady and St. James."—G. P. Hammond, *Don Juan de Oñate and the Founding of New Mexico* (Historical Society of New Mexico, *Publications in History*, vol. 2, October 1927), p. 204. It appears that Dr. Espinosa is thus trying to interpret the de Vargas statement: "Our Lady of the Conquest . . . who is the one that was saved from the fury of the savages."

by those who read in the *Journals* that Our Lady on the Standard had led the soldiers in the attack.

But now we know with certainty that there was such a statue present during the battle for Santa Fe. Very likely it was not carried into battle, since de Vargas himself, who seems to omit nothing concerning his Lady in the *Journals*, failed to write anything to that effect, and also because the traditions are contradictory in this respect. The one that has come down to our day asserts that the statue did go into the fray, whereas the one current in 1806 leads one to believe that it was enshrined at the civilian camp, which is thought to have been located on the sheltered site of the present Rosario cemetery, while the military encampment overlooked the country in all directions on one of the higher hills north of the town. When petitioning the Bishop of Durango for permission to erect the Rosario chapel, on June 29, 1806, Fr. Francisco de Hozio described the site as "the place where the holy Image was placed at the time of the second conquest of this Kingdom."[42]

As noted previously, no other description or even mention of a statue is known from the Aguilar entry in the Inventory of 1697 to the Domínguez and Candelaria writings of 1777. The next one is found in the Rosario Inventory of 1796, and then in Fr. Hozio's petition of 1806, both of them already quoted; mention of the bejeweled statue is also made by the Custos, Fr. Benito Pereyro, in his 1808 report, and one of the latest "old descriptions" is that of Father DeFouri in 1887. All in all, the documentary evidence is quite plentiful.

Next comes the identification of the statue now pre-

---

42. AASF, no. 52, *Tipton Transcriptions.* This is a small note tablet in which are copied a few brief documents filling six pages, and on page 7 is this statement: "The foregoing document is a correct copy made by me from a correct copy of an original, which original was in the possession of Rev. Antonio Fourchegu, Vicar General of the Archdiocese of Santa Fe, New Mexico, on August 26, 1911, on which date he loaned said original to me; thereupon I made from said original the correct copy from which the foregoing, on the first six consecutive leaves, was correctly copied by me on March 25, 1917. [Signed] Will M. Tipton. Santa Fe, N. M., April 2, 1917. Witness: [Signed] Alice Stevens Tipton."

These originals cannot be found in the Archives of the Archdiocese. Mons. Fourchegu very likely found these papers, together with a painting of St. Francis and other items, in the Rosario chapel itself.

served in the Cathedral as Our Lady of the Rosary, *La Conquistadora*. The head, at least, and very likely the entire body, are carved out of willow wood.[43] She is twenty-eight inches tall from her foot to the crown of her head. Old-timers say that she was taller. One can see where the base at some time was sawed off right through the faces of three cherubs at her feet, the lower halves being cleverly restored and connected with a new gilt board-base which is bolted onto a palanquin for processions. What was cut off was most likely a mass of clouds resting on a small rococo pedestal, such as may be seen under ancient Spanish and Latin-American statues—for example, *Nuestra Señora del Rosario de Talpa*, here reproduced. This must have made her some six inches taller, if we recall the eye-measurements of Fr. Gómez in 1686 and Fr. Domínguez in 1777, both of whom stated that she was thirty-three inches high "and a little more." When the act of vandalism was perpetrated we do not know. Monsignor Antonio Fourchegu, Rector of the Cathedral from 1892 until 1920, declared that the lower base was sawed off by a carpenter to fit her into a niche. Fr. Barnabas Meyer, O.F.M., has notes on the matter which he took down in the early twenties, sometime before the Monsignor's death.

What with continual rough handling through a couple of centuries of frequent dressing and undressing, let alone the hacking and sawing done in two or more instances, the image was in a sorry state in 1930, when a real artist, Gustave Baumann of Santa Fe, began a careful restoration. The face itself, which is modeled in yeso and not carved from the wood of the head, was brittle and ready to fall off, except for the small areas around the eyes and mouth; some of the fingers were broken off; the tip of the bent right

---

43. A projecting sliver from behind the left ear was sent to Fr. Herculan Kolinski, O.F.M., of Cincinnati, an expert on wood, who in turn consulted with Dr. H. Muegel, dendrologist of the University of Cincinnati. Microscopic examination reveals that it is definitely willow wood, and just as definitely not cottonwood, as Dr. Muegel suspected at first. However, since the many species of willow grow in every part of the globe, and since they are most difficult to distinguish among themselves, even when the whole tree is present, this identification does not help us at all in establishing the country (whether Spain, Michoacán, or Guatemala) where the statue might have been made.

knee had also been sliced off, evidently by the same man who sawed off the base to fit her into a glass niche. Then, Mr. Baumann writes,

> After removing the old base which was a white pine plank, I found the base of the statue to have been sawed off to fit— A round plug in the base proved to be the end of a standard that extended into the hollow center, from which I surmise that La Conquistadora was probably brought in with the standard resting on a stirrup, which seems perfectly logical to me. A scrap of white woolen cloth was all I found inside. This was replaced. If it ever contained some sort of record it was probably removed at the time the arms were made moveable and the base cut off. I just did not have the heart to leave those cherubs cut in half, so they were restored. I think the Rectory was disappointed I did not restore the arms, but it would have left less of the original than you have now, also it would not have been possible to dress, which I think is an important outlet of interest to the parish.
>
> The face had been repainted many times (not too skillfully) and broke away since the glue-size underneath had disintegrated—all excepting the eyes and lips. I lost several sleepless nights getting her back to her old self—also I gave her several new fingers which I imagine can't stand pulling through the sleeves too well.

The plug which Mr. Baumann surmised to be the end of a "standard" was more likely a wooden pin fitting the statue and pedestal together, their line of juncture being hidden by molded clouds of yeso painted over. The artist also told me that he partly repaired the mutilated knee; the underlying wood, he thought at the time, might be some kind of mahogany, though he was not sure. In 1933, Mr. Baumann also made an imagined replica of the statue as it might have looked originally, which, since then, has been enshrined on the Cathedral terrace during the annual Santa Fe Fiesta. (The original, however, is still carried every year in the traditional procession to and from the Rosario Chapel.)

When she is stripped of her clothing, the fine craftsmanship of some nameless *santero* of old becomes at once apparent. From the waist down to the feet, about thirteen inches, the wood is finely carved into a long tunic partly overlapped by a mantle. The same workmanship is also partly discernible on the back all the way up to the shoulders. The wood was first covered with yeso, then with a red pigment. What remains of the tunic, at the lower left, has a thick gold-leafed brocade-effect on the red base, while the mantle is solid gold-leaf, with a one-and-one-half-inch border in blue with gold brocade, edged on the inside with a thin quarter-inch line of orange and gold. The cherub heads (and hers, too, before mutilation) seem to have been painted in natural colors, the hair being gold-leaf shaded with brown.

From the waist up to the neck, the effect is not so pleasing. Her middle is gouged into a wasp-waist which rises up in a squarish flat-chested torso, to which are attached long puppet-arms, both articulated at the shoulders and elbows. At first sight, one is tempted to curse the fiend who did the mutilating. But the fact that this formless upper portion of the torso is covered with rough linen tightly glued, according to the known practice of ancient saint-makers, and that the whole is painted with a red pigment similar to that under the gold-leaf further down—all this makes one pause. However, because traces of the carved and painted dress remain on the back above the waist and on the head, the conclusion to be drawn is that the statue was at first beautifully carved throughout, and not originally meant to be dressed. At the same time, the antique appearance of the puppet-arms transformation and the fact that dresses were put on as early as 1684, and even before that, lead one to believe that this change took place sometime in the seventeenth century before 1680.

The face is indeed beautiful, with small mouth, and eyes, and a thin nose, the result of a good restoration performed on the disfigurements perpetrated by amateurs through the centuries. There is nothing doll-like or mushily sentimental about it, like most modern statues. It is a queenly face, conscious of majesty, yet not at all haughty, staring straight into a world we cannot see. Although the features are not quite anatomically correct, as a whole they appear perfect. Recalling Fr. Domínguez's statement in 1777 that "although old it is newly retouched," and the Rev. James DeFouri's in 1887 that "repairs have spoiled the natural beauty of her face," makes one all the more thankful for the propitious appearance in 1930 of Gustave Baumann's understanding heart and skillful hands.

But the rest of the head, now fortunately hidden by the wig, shows ugly signs of unskilled and reckless hacking, leaving the willow wood grimly exposed. As can be plainly discerned, the original carved locks framing her face were parted in the middle and flowed down to the shoulders, revealing only the lobes of her ears. The same mantle that shows below the waist on her right, and discernible in spots on the back, shoulders, and head, covered the head completely from the rear. Then someone decided that a wig of human hair would look better. Off came practically all of the carved hair and the mantle, while a deep shelf was gouged above her brow, the better to anchor the crude wig. Again the temptation is to incriminate her devotees of the Victorian era. But in 1777, Fr. Domínguez mentions a wig which was never removed—for obvious reasons. Then, just below the ear-lobes, two perforated iron wedges are hammered in, for the purpose of holding ear-rings, of which she had several pairs already in 1686;[44] since these had to be attached somehow, it may be that these wedges or something similar were there already at that time.

As for her dresses and underclothing, over and above her jewelry and other valuables, one marvels at the quality of the cloth used, materials which were costly and difficult to get in those days of poverty and dangerous existence in this isolated frontier of a then unexplored continent. The lists reproduced later on speak for themselves. None of these articles has survived. During the past century the dresses put on her took the flat-chested, rear-bustle Victorian look of the times, a style which has been kept up for her until now. The old regal brocades with their royal effect of former centuries disappeared not only physically but from the stunted imagination of the people as well. This year new dresses are being made from old and modern brocades in the original style; and these will be used as patterns when her devotees wish to donate new dresses as their forebears have done for centuries.

---

44. Inventory, f. 10v.

*Left: The Baumann restoration, which shows the Benavides
"Assumption"*
Right: Original statue, undraped, front view

Left: Original statue, undraped, rear view (photo by Robert Martin)
Right: Our Lady of Talpa, shown for comparison

A word about the Child in her arms. As far back as anyone recalls, her flexible arms have been empty. Yet in older Church iconography, Our Lady of the Rosary was never properly represented unless she held the Christ-Child. The latter is not mentioned as being with her in any of the old descriptions; undoubtedly, He is taken for granted, as, for example, by Fr. Domínguez, who omits mention of Him in describing the Lady but writes later on in listing her wardrobe: "Two little white dresses for the Child Jesus of the Lady."[45] Now, there was a small Infant in the Cathedral Museum which could well be the *"Niño Jesus de la Señora."* It is yeso-covered wood and painted in natural colors; despite its small size—about six inches—it must have been considered very precious in bygone days, for it wears finely-wrought shoes of pure gold. Restored to the Lady's arms, it proves to be somewhat small in proportion to her figure, but the proportions are no different from those seen in other ancient Spanish Madonnas—again, for example, the Lady of the Rosary of Talpa. Further, the Lady's puppet arms and hands, poised very awkwardly when empty, now hold the Child and exhibit a rosary most gracefully, as they were meant to do.

Without any doubt, the image treasured in the Santa Fe Parroquia from time immemorial, in whose honor a yearly celebration has been most faithfully kept because of the popular belief that it was brought by de Vargas at the time of the Reconquest, is the very same one which the Rosary Confraternity venerated at San Lorenzo. The tradition that claims that she came with de Vargas is correct, but the *Reconquistador* himself tells us that this was but a return of a Queen to her former throne, from which she had been rescued from the fury of the Indian rebels. He also tells us that she was the Patroness of the whole Kingdom of New Mexico and of its capital, as may be also seen from the devotion expressed by all and sundry in the early accounts.

The main question remaining is: When and where was the statue made, and when did it come to New Mexico? Certainly it was not called *"La Conquistadora"* because of the

45. *Op. cit.*

Reconquest. The feeling brought on by this accumulated wealth of testimony is that it was brought by the pioneer friars or colonists, the *conquistadores*, between the years 1600 and 1650, especially since we know that the Rosary Confraternity was functioning during Governor Manso's term in 1656-1659. Before concluding this chapter, then, we might well speculate upon some interesting references in other early seventeenth century documents in an attempt to peer behind the curtain of the past.

In both of his famous *Memorials*, Fr. Alonso de Benavides wrote of a beautiful statue of the Virgin in Santa Fe, in the church of the Spaniards, which had impressed some visiting Apache chieftains—"an image in the round of the Assumption of the Virgin Our Lady, which I had carried there, and stood well-adorned in a chapel. . . ." (1630)— "an image of the Assumption of Our Lady which I had placed in a chapel in the church of Santa Fe where the Spaniards worshipped" (1634).[46] The first time, Fr. Benavides states that he himself had brought the statue. This same Padre, as newly-elected Custos, had signed a receipt for a statue of the Virgin down in Mexico City before coming up to New Mexico in 1625; it was brought in the largest recorded consignment of goods that came to the New Mexico Missions in that period, and in the same wagon train that brought Fr. Benavides and eleven other Franciscans. Although the statue itself is not described, we know of its size from the crate in which it was packed, a "case in which the Virgin went, a *vara* and a quarter long and three-quarters wide and two-thirds high."[47] No other statue of the Virgin is mentioned among the many other images entered in the lengthy *Contaduría* records extant for the period. If

---

46. E. E. Ayer, *The Memorial of Fray Alonso de Benavides, 1630* (Chicago, 1916), p. 155; F. W. Hodge, *Fray Alonso de Benavides' Revised Memorial of 1634* (Albuquerque, 1945), p. 91.

I have used the word "Assumption" for "*Tránsito*" in the originals, which others have translated as the "death" of the Virgin. Their translation is correct literally, but wrong liturgically. In employing the word "Tránsito," Fr. Benavides, by metonymy, was merely using one of the three ideas celebrated in the title and feast of the Assumption: The Death or Passing Away of Mary, her Assumption into Heaven, and her Coronation.

47. A. G. I., *Contaduría*, leg. 726, Data.

we take the *vara* to be about thirty-three inches, the crate was about forty inches long, twenty-four inches wide, and twenty-two inches high. The *Conquistadora* statue would fit quite snugly into such a box, with enough inches to spare all around for protective packing. Identification of the latter with the Benavides Virgin is rather far-fetched, it is true, but the possibility and even probability of such a thing cannot be lightly dismissed. Between Fr. Benavides' departure from New Mexico in 1629 to the decade preceding Governor Manso's term, many things could have happened to the statue, like the gouging of its chest and the addition of puppet-arms for dressing, and a change of name.

Here is a deduction which, if proved certain someday, would not surprise me at all. The original Parroquia of Santa Fe, the mud hut which Fr. Benavides found in 1625, was dedicated in honor of Mary's Assumption; the statue that he brought represented the Assumption; the new substantial Parroquia that was built during his term as Custos, and in which he enshrined the statue, was most likely entitled "of the Assumption," since the new church merely supplanted the older inadequate structure. (Decades later the Parroquia was referred to as "of the Conception.") It is the period in which the Spanish inhabitants there are referred to, as they were later on by their children and grandchildren, as *conquistadores*. Then, thirty years later, a Confraternity of Our Lady of the Rosary is already existing there. Now, Baumann's replica, faithfully and logically following the obvious leads in the gouged upper portion of the old statue, is an unmistakable representation of the Assumption—especially the clouds and cherubs bearing up the lightly poised figure and the ecstatic character of the face and eyes. (The only mistake on his part is that he did not cross both hands about the wrists on her breast, simply because for this he had no lead.) Next, this posing of the lone figure on clouds and cherubs is not characteristic of the traditional representation of Our Lady of the Rosary, but rather that of the Assumption or Immaculate Conception. The deduction, then, is that our so-called "de Vargas statue" may be none other than the Benavides statue of the *Assumption* which he brought in 1625 to the Santa Fe Parroquia of the same name, the principal and only parish church of the Spaniards for more than a century. Sometime during the next thirty years a Rosary Confraternity was founded which adopted the "Patroness of the Kingdom and its *Villa* of Santa Fe" as its visible rallying point; in that period, or in the decades prior to the 1680 Indian Revolt, the little statue was mutilated and the puppet-arms were attached, in order that she might be dressed as "Our Lady of the Rosary" holding an Infant and a rosary. Since no wig is mentioned in the 1685-1726 fragments, and since it is first described in 1777 and the mutilation of the head appears much more recent than the puppet-arms transformation, the head must have been hacked and the wig first attached during the Confraternity's second phase of 1770. Therefore, while referring to her as *Nuestra Señora del Rosario* because their Rosary Confraternity revolved around it, the pre-Revolt inhabitants also remembered her as one who had come in the days of their pioneer forebears and called her, in addition, *"La Conquistadora."*

CHAPTER III

THE LADY CHAPELS

1. The "Conquistadora Chapel."

Should the "Benavides-statue" theory prove to be correct, the first chapel of La Conquistadora as an image of the Assumption was the original parish church of Santa Fe, built sometime after 1610, the one that appeared like a mud-hut to Fr. Benavides on his arrival in 1625; from there the statue was transferred to a special chapel in Benavides' new Parroquia, finished by 1628 or 1629, and presumably in this same chapel she was transformed into a Lady of the Rosary years later in the manner and under the circumstances previously described.

But even if La Conquistadora were an altogether different statue of identical size, since the Rosary Confraternity already existed in 1656-1659, the first Conquistadora chapel would still be the Parroquia itself, or else the military chapel attached to the Palace of the Governors. The only reference that might apply here, and this only for the Indian Revolt period, occurs in the description of the siege of Santa Fe in 1680. When definite rumblings of an Indian uprising were felt in the Capital, its citizens, as well as others from the surrounding settlements and ranches, fortified themselves within the town. On August 13, the Indians in full force laid siege to Santa Fe. By degrees they captured parts of the town, forcing the Spaniards to retreat at last into the large walled military compound within the Palace of the Governors; the people had most likely removed what they could of value from the Parroquia, which was soon destroyed by the enemy, who also set fire to San Miguel Church. Several counter-attacks in the name of the Virgin were made by the Spaniards, which inflicted severe casualties on the Indians, but they found themselves unable to break the siege. Wrote Governor Otermín:

Proceeding to the use of arms, they began to fight, taking possession of the church of the *villa* and of the houses, setting fire alike to the holy temple and to the said houses, burning everything. . . . They came to set fire to the doors of a hermitage of Our Lady which is in the tower of the said *casas reales* [the Palace of the Governors], where, seeing that they could not overcome us, they occupied the river and the houses, cutting off our water entirely for a period of two days and a night.[48]

Unable to hold out any longer, since the people of the Rio Abajo had not come to his aid, Otermín sallied forth with his subjects on August 21, the men defending the women and children, the aged and wounded, in their midst. With them went *La Conquistadora*, "saved from the fury of the savages," but we do not know with certainty whether her old throne at the time had been in the Parroquia, from which she had been taken to the Palace during the siege, or whether her own shrine at this period was "the hermitage of Our Lady" in the tower-chapel. During the thirteen-year exile, as the early fragment sheets point out, her shrine was the chapel in the *Real* of San Lorenzo, named in honor of the Saint on whose Feast, as Fr. Ayeta wrote, the Indians had rebelled and massacred so many of the Spaniards.[49]

During the first crucial days of the 1693 Reconquest, the statue was still enclosed in a wagon, which was apparently · kept in the civilian camp on the site of the present Rosario cemetery. Meanwhile, de Vargas looked around the *Villa* for a building in which Mass could be said and in which his vow could be kept to enthrone the Lady of the Conquest, as he mentioned in October in his letter to the Viceroy. First he examined the Parroquia; it was beyond repair. Next, he ordered the San Miguel chapel re-roofed, but the Indians protested with reason that, winter having set in, it was too cold to cut and haul *vigas* from the mountains. These Indians in turn offered him a tower in the Palace which had been used by them as a kiva. Overcoming the protests of the friars with good arguments, he reopened the original entrance, which the Indians had sealed up years before, and designated this place as the temporary parish church. Then

---

48. C. W. Hackett and C. C. Shelby, *Revolt of the Pueblo Indians of New Mexico*, (Coronado Historical Series, VIII, Albuquerque, 1942), I, 113.
49. Anne E. Hughes, *op. cit.*, p. 316.

came the days of waiting for the Indians to move to their Pueblos, their sudden resistance, the battle for Santa Fe, the Spanish victory, and the repossession by the colonists of the ancient capital. Then, most likely, *La Conquistadora* returned to the "hermitage of Our Lady," and perhaps remained there until the Parroquia was finished more than two decades later. Since, all this while (between 1693 and 1717), succeeding Governors were also *mayordomos* of the Confraternity, the Palace chapel was her logical resting place.

The new Parroquia, dedicated after the Reconquest in honor of San Francisco de Asís, facing the street of the same name, was a-building during the second decade of the new century. Records of this period of rehabilitation and reapportioning of property in Santa Fe bear witness to both the time and the location.[50] From the old *Conquistadora* sheets we learn that the Confraternity itself was still established at the Palace of the Governors in March 17, 1714. But by October of 1717, it was "In this church of the *Villa* of Santa Fe," and in October of the following year a more explicit term is used: "In this church of Our Holy Father St. Francis of the *Villa* of Santa Fe,"[51] which shows that the main part was finished and in use by that time. The Confraternity's own chapel, attached to the Parroquia, also appears to have been completed. Between October 16 and sometime in December, 1717, the *mayordomo*, Bernardo de Sena, paid sixty pesos to the carpenter Juan de Medina for building the high altar of the chapel, as well as its sacristy.[52] He also paid another sum to Andrés Montoya for hauling lumber for the sacristy, and still another to Salvador Archuleta for thirty-five *vigas* (no exact date given) ; these entries follow others of March, 1718, but very likely the timbers had been cut and hauled the preceding October before winter set in, or even before the carpenter was paid for his work. At any rate, we can safely say that the Lady-Chapel,

---

50. *Sp. Arch.*, I, No. 181 (1714), "*la Yglesia nueba q se esta fabricando.*" Also, nos. 491, 498, 680, 1072, and 1074.
51. (d) Accounts, f. 2. (e) Minutes, both sides.
52. Accounts, f. 63v.

connecting with the north transept wall of the Parroquia, was already in use by the spring of 1718. Nor is there any doubt that this chapel is the North Chapel attached to the present Cathedral. Documentary testimony from its erection until now is continuous. Besides the old Confraternity fragments of 1713-1726, we have the oldest extant burial register of the Parroquia, listing the burials made inside the new church and the location of each grave.[53] Starting with March, 1726, the following persons, probably leading members of the Confraternity and members of their families, found a last resting place in the North Chapel:

Maria Hurtado, March 22, 1726, widow of Antonio Montoya, buried *"en la Capilla de Ntra Señora."* Sebastián Gonzales, husband of Lucía Ortiz, June 11, 1726, buried *"en la Capilla de Ntra Señora."* Tomasa Gonzales, wife of Don Bernardino de Sena, Feb. 20, 1727, buried in the sanctuary of *"La Capilla de Ntra. Sra."* Gerónima Barela, widow of José Domínguez, April 11, 1727, *"en la Capilla de nuestra Señora."* Margarita Martín, wife of Juan de Apodaca, April 25, 1727, *"en la Capilla de Ntra Señora."*

"El Regidor Don Salvador Montoya," May 8, 1727, in the sanctuary of *"la capilla de Ntra Señora La Conquistadora."* Tomasa Montoya, wife of Alfonso Rael de Aguilar, May 20, 1727, under the high altar of *"la Capilla de Ntra Señora."* (Burials in outside cemetery begin May 19, 1732.)

Domingo Tenorio, eight years old, June 8, 1733, *"en la Capilla de Nta. Señora."* Manuela Gonzales, infant, June 10, 1733, *"en la Capilla de Nstra Sra. la Conquistadora."* Francisca Ygnacia, ten years old, June 7, 1733, *"en la Capilla de N. Sra. la Conquistadora."* Gertrudis, six years old, June 16, 1733, *"en la Capilla de Ntra. Señora."* Felipe Sánchez, eighty, Feb. 1, 1734, *"en la Capilla de N. Sra. La Conquistadora."*

Don Alonso Rael de Aguilar, April 10, 1735, in the *"Capilla de la Virgen."* María Dorotea, infant, June 24, 1733, *"en la Capilla de Nra. Sra."* Simona Domínguez, Nov. 20, 1736, and Angela Gertrudis Valdés, Jan. 30, 1737, *"en la Capilla de Nra. Señora."*

Doña Teodora García, wife of the *Teniente General* Don Juan Páez

---

53. AASF, Burial-48, *Santa Fé*. Compare these names with those in the fragments. The *Auto de Presentación*, January 6, 1726, states that it is the third book of burials. Its lost predecessors no doubt contained the funerals conducted from the Palace tower-chapel and San Miguel, as also some from the newly-finished Parroquia until the second book was filled up to January of 1726. If we had the two older burial books, the last resting place of de Vargas would be no longer a mystery.

Hurtado, Nov. 17, 1736, in the sanctuary of the *"Capilla de Ntra Señ-ora."* Doña Manuela García, widow (of Salvador Montoya) in the same grave as her sister, the same day. Francisca de Ribera, maiden, Dec. 22, 1737, *"en la Capilla de Ntra Sra la Conquistadora."* Juan Rodríguez, *Alcalde Mayor* of the *Villa*, Jan. 2, 1738, *"en la Capilla de N. Sra."* Domingo Fernando Tenorio, child, May 17, 1738, *"en la Capilla de Ntra Sra la Conquistadora."* Juan Lucero, Nov. 23, 1741, *"en la Capilla de Ntra Sra la Conquistadora."* Benito Domínguez, April 5, 1742, *"en la Capilla de Nra. Sra."*

"El Theniente Genl Dn Juan Paez Hurtado". . . May 5, 1742 . . . *"en el Altar de Ntra Sra la Conquistadora."* Don José de Reaño, husband of Doña María de Ruibal, April 16, 1743, *"en la Capilla de N.a Sa. del Rosario."* (Up to this time Fr. Guerrero had used the term *"Conquista-dora,"* but from now on other friars write *"Rosario."* Also, after this last date, no mention is made of the exact place of burial until the 1770's, after the revival of the Confraternity.)

The child José Bernardo, July 18, 1776, *"a el entrar de la Puerta de la Capilla de Na Sa del Rosario,"* entry by Fr. Francisco Atanasio Domín-guez. He also buried María Ygnacia Romero, July 28, 1776, *"en la capilla de N.S. del Rosario de esta Yglesia de N.P.S. Fran.co de esta Villa de Sta. Fe."*

Juana Teresa, child, Dec. 30, 1776, *"a la entrada de la Capilla de N.S. del Rosario."* Juan Esteban Ortiz, soldier killed by Comanches, buried Nov. 17, 1777, in the Parish Church of St. Francis, *"en frente de la Capilla de Nuestra Sa del Rosario."* Maria Francisca Rivera, April 25, 1778, inside the Parroquia *"en la Capilla de Nra Señora del Rosario."* Manuela Roibal, May 1, 1778, in the Parroquia *"en la Capilla de Na Sa del Rosario."* The last two recorded burials are: Catarina Rivera, Feb. 31 (*sic*), 1779, and José de Dimas, May 21, 1780, in the Parroquia, *"en la Capilla de Ntra Sa de Rosario."*

The earliest full description of the chapel found so far is that of Fr. Atanasio Domínguez in 1777.[54]

CAPILLA DEL ROSARIO

To speak with more order and propriety I reserved this chapel for this place. Well, it is located on the Gospel side of the principal Church against the outer wall of the Transept [extending] towards the out-side as is the chapel of Suleta in the Church of our convent of Mexico. It is made of adobes, thick walls of about a *vara;* its doorway is opened archwise in the wall of said place, and from there to the wall of the high altar it is twenty *varas* long, seven wide, and nine high.

---

54. *Op. cit.*, ff. 4128-4133.

Its *vigas* are laid evenly and without skylight like the church, and they are twenty-four new ones, round (like those of the transept in the Church) and laid over the ancient corbels. Its sanctuary is distinguished [from the nave] by two small steps going up, and the top one measures four *varas* towards the center, being as wide as the nave of the body of the chapel. Its choir is located over the doorway of its orientation on twelve projecting corbels, with its small railing or balcony; its depth is three *varas*, and its width that of the chapel. The floor has new joists. The entrance is double-doored and of planed planks, high and wide in proportion, and has bolts. Its windows are two, on the Epistle side at an even distance, with wooden grill-work, and facing the east. Its furnishing or adornment is as follows:

HIGH ALTAR

There is no altar-screen, but a large niche which rests on a bench for the purpose, and two bases on the sides of the niche with two small niches on them (these and the large one are like little chapels), make up for it—and all painted red with yellow mouldings as though in tempera. . . . [*Next follows the description of the statue already quoted.*] Concerning its valuable ornaments more will be said anon, and thus there will be no confusion as to which it has on, the rest remaining put away with the exception of what I mentioned as her wearing all the time.

The niches on the bases have their small Saints in the round, and proportionately distributed on the walls to the Sanctuary are ten canvases in oil without frames, and four on elkskin, all large, and with various Saints; and equally spaced among these, twenty small canvases. The altar-table is of wood, movable, and dressed with what is necessary, even to a platform and rug; with attention to the fact that the frontal is of wood in relief, and painted like the aforesaid niches. The interior view of this chapel is really gay [*alegrita*].

NAVE

In it are two altars; the one on the Gospel side is of the Blood of Christ with large Crucifix in the round, very beautiful, before a canopy of silk, already old, and at the Lord's feet the Sorrowful Mother in the round about a *vara* tall, and dressed; and to one side of this Lady a small-sized Lord St. Joseph, carved. The altar-table is of wood, dressed like the high altar, even to a rug over the platform. The other altar is on the Epistle side, and is [dedicated] to St. John Nepomucene; Father Cuéllar erected it, and through the use of his donation the titular Saint was acquired, which is carved, three *cuartas* tall, in a niche painted with colors in tempera, and six large colored plates spread over the outside, reredos-style. The altar-table is of wood, dressed like the aforesaid others. The frontal is of painted panel; and the small rug was also paid for from the donation of said Father, together with the Saint and his niche and the plates. The rest belongs to this chapel. This altar has a lower gradine, and on it are a carved St. Anthony of Padua, small, and two Child-Jesus' of varnish-compound. In this chapel is founded a Confraternity with title of the Rosary, and about this as soon as I finish with an account of the SACRISTY.

This sacristy is described as running east from the chapel on the Epistle side, "a little lower than the sanctuary." Therefore the door leading into it is the present one opening to the outside. Then follow long lists of vestments, linens, dresses, sacred vessels, and all things pertaining to the Confraternity. Fr. Domínguez ends with one last word on the latter, namely, that he has had a hard time seeking in vain for papers of canonical erection, as also for those of the Confraternity of the Blessed Sacrament, adding that the matter is pending before the Sacred Curia of Durango.

Other brief early descriptions of this chapel are those of Fr. Morfí in 1782, Antonio José Ortiz in 1797 and 1805, Fr. Pereyro in 1808, and Vicario Fernández in 1826. In the latter part of the century, Fray Agustín Morfí visited the Franciscan Missions of the northern provinces of New Spain, but did not reach New Mexico; hence his information is second-hand. Concerning Santa Fe, he wrote: "In la Calle Real and to the East is the parish Church consecrated to N.P.S. Francisco and in it is a chapel dedicated to N.S. del Sagrario under the protection of La Conquistadora."[55]

Don Antonio José Ortiz, a pious old wealthy citizen of Santa Fe, carried on an eight-year correspondence with Bishop Olivares of Durango concerning private chapels for himself and his own restoration of the Parroquia, which had fallen into ruin around 1798. In a letter of January 25, 1805, after telling the Bishop how he had rebuilt and enlarged the Parroquia, the whole body of which had fallen down "six years ago," he mentions having renovated the altar and the sanctuary—and the chapel of Nuestra Señora del Rosario.[56]

55. Alfred B. Thomas, Forgotten Frontiers (University of Oklahoma, 1932), p. 91. Sagrario, instead of Rosario, is either a mistake of Fr. Morfí or a misreading by the translator, or else whoever was the informant of Fr. Morfí had the Confraternity of the Blessed Sacrament in mind "under the protection" of that of La Conquistadora.

56. José D. Sena, "The Chapel of Don Antonio José Ortiz," NEW MEXICO HISTORICAL REVIEW, XIII, 347-359. I have not yet encountered these letters in the Archives of the Archdiocese.

He is the man who, according to the Candelaria *Noticias*, offered himself as perennial *mayordomo*. A report made by the Custos, Fray Benito Pereyro, in December, 1808, states that annexed to the Parish Church of Santa Fe there are two chapels, one of them in honor of Our Lady of the Rosary, this being *La Conquistadora*.[57] One of the Vicars General of Durango who now and then were making juridical Visitations to the Church in New Mexico was Don Agustín Fernández San Vicente. He wrote in 1826: "Inside, communicating with the transept, are two large separate chapels, the one on the north side dedicated to *N.S. del Rosario*, called · also *La Conquistadora*."[58]

As previously pointed out, here is more than ample testimony for the existence of the *"Conquistadora* Chapel" from the time the post-Reconquest Parroquia was finished, around 1717, through every decade to our own day. By historical association, if not by direct statement, all this also bears witness to the *Conquistadora's* identity, as the selfsame statue first mentioned in 1686 and still venerated today, as it has been through so many generations, in the Parroquia of Santa Fe.

One last word on this particular chapel. What we see today attached to the north chancel section of the Lamy Cathedral is only the outer half of the longer structure described by Domínguez, as one can see from old photographs of the exterior taken in the middle of the last century.[59] Two windows had been opened in the west wall at this latter period. The stone Cathedral, built by Archbishop Lamy around the adobe Parroquia, is much wider, and so its lateral naves, in connecting with the old side

George Kubler, *The Religious Architecture of New Mexico in the Colonial Period and Since the American Occupation* (Colorado Springs, 1940), p. 22, footnote. Readings by Stallings in 1937 show age of vigas to be 1745 plus or minus and 1851 plus. Cf. Domínguez description of chapel interior.

57. *Sp. Arch.*, I, No. 1191.

58. The original, according to Salpointe, is in the "church records," but I have not seen it in the Archives. *Soldiers of the Cross* (Banning, California, 1898), p. 160. Quoted also by Kubler, *op. cit.*, p. 101, and Twitchell, *Leading Facts of New Mexican History* (Cedar Rapids, 1912), II, 166, footnote.

59. Museum of New Mexico prints reproduced in Prince, *Mission Churches*, and in *The Santa Fe Cathedral* (Santa Fe, 1947), a popular illustrated guide to the Cathedral.

Above: The old Parroquia, on the site of which the present-day Cathedral of Saint Francis stands. The Conquistadora Chapel, built in 1717 and now incorporated into the Cathedral, may be seen at the left

Below: The original Rosario Chapel of 1807, built on the traditional site of de Vargas' encampment, as it appeared shortly before the present-day nave was added in 1914

chapels, took off their inner sections. The statue of *La Conquistadora* has been restored to her rightful place in her chapel, and little is needed, over and above permission from the authorities, to remodel its altar and sanctuary in the style of the period.

2. The "Rosario Chapel."

Distinct from the *"Conquistadora* Chapel," even in popular terminology, is the lone structure which stands in the Rosario cemetery in the northwest section of Santa Fe. Not many years ago it stood well away from the town limits. It is this particular building, and not the North Chapel of the Parroquia, which has been associated with the latter-day phase of the *Conquistadora* legend—that de Vargas had vowed to build a chapel on that very spot and hold a yearly procession thither. As for this part of the tradition, the *Reconquistador* makes no mention of such a vow; devoted as he was to the Blessed Virgin Mary, filling the pages of his *Journals* with her name on less important occasions, he surely would have recorded such a momentous act on his part, especially since he was *mayordomo* of her Confraternity at the time and had expressed his intention of returning the New Mexicans' Madonna to her former throne. Moreover, no chapel is known to have existed there until the first decade of the last century.

On June 29, 1806, Fray Francisco de Hozio, for many years military chaplain of the *Castrense* and at this time interim pastor of the secularized Santa Fe Parroquia, petitioned the Bishop of Durango for permission to erect a chapel of "Our Lady of the Holy Rosary at the place where the holy Image was placed at the time of the second conquest of this Kingdom. . . ."[60] It is well to note here how this Padre speaks of two separate conquests by de Vargas. Most likely Father Hozio was unaware, like the rest of the people from whom he learned the tradition, of the two distinct Reconquests of 1692 and 1693. In mentioning a second conquest, he was voicing the popular tradition of two conquests

---

60. AASF. See Note 41.

in one and the same year—in fact, in the same month. The first was the triumphant entry into Santa Fe, and the second was the battle that took place some days later after the Tanos refused to evacuate the town and defied the Spaniards.

Here we have a clue as to where the statue of Our Lady of the Conquest, "who was enclosed in a wagon," was kept between December 18 and 31, and where she waited while that other image of hers, the Remedios *painting* on the royal standard, led the troops on the assault. It would be most logical to believe that during the battle the women in the civilian camp, with such men as were not in the battle, unpacked the statue and set it up in a makeshift shrine while they prayed for victory. This would be in line with what Don José D. Sena remembers hearing from his fore-bears—that, prior to the erection of this chapel, a shrine of cottonwood and juniper branches was erected every year for the Rosario processions and novena of Masses.[61]

Exactly when this chapel was begun and completed is not certain. The Bishop of Durango granted the Hozio petition in a letter of July 29, 1806, with permission for an ordinary priest to bless it when finished; he also stated that Mass might be celebrated in it, and the Sacraments of Penance and Holy Eucharist administered, by any secular or religious priest having the ordinary diocesan faculties. "Let the chapel be constructed as directed, Santa Fe, October 6, 1806," reads an annotation to the Bishop's letter by Real Alencaster, Governor of New Mexico.[62] If begun after this date, or the following spring (as is more likely), the small building was finished by the fall of 1807. On August 31, 1808, Antonio Ortiz, as *Mayordomo* of the 1770 Confraternity, wrote the Governor regarding the general collection of dues during the month of June in Santa Fe and surrounding districts, "for the cult and adornment of the new chapel of *N.S. del Rosario*, who is venerated as *Conquistadora* of this Province in this Parish Church. . . ."[63] "The new chapel" clearly refers to the one in question, while the object

61. "De Vargas Procession," *Santa Fe New Mexican*, June 30, 1933, p. 4, c. 6-7.
62. AASF. See Note 41.
63. *Sp. Arch.*, II, No. 2151.

that gives it its name of *Rosario* is the statue known as *Conquistadora* in the north chapel of the Parroquia.

The faculties granted by the Bishop in 1806 were renewed by Don Juan Bautista Ladrón de Guevara, Visitor General, when he visited Santa Fe on April 28, 1818. The chapel was likewise examined and approved by the Vicar General of Durango, Don Agustín Fernández San Vicente, on September 7, 1826. On September 22, 1833, Bishop Zubiría, while on visitation, approved and renewed the foregoing grants, provided that the traditional devotion to the Holy Mother was kept up. This last action by the Bishop explains the temporary resurgence of zeal in the 1782 Confraternity book for this period.[64]

The Rosario Chapel faced south, with a porched sacristy extension to the rear on the east side. Without doubt it was built in the native "Santa Fe-Pueblo" style of the times; but in later years, sometime during the American occupation, and before 1913, it had acquired a white lime coating and a brick cornice in the so-called "Territorial" style of the period, as may be seen in an old photograph in Prince's book. This author, who believed that an older chapel had existed there before this one, says that the picture was taken the day before work was started on the new addition in 1914. This latter was done under the supervision of Monsignor Fourchegu, Rector of the Cathedral, who had this much larger addition built directly into the east lateral wall of the old chapel, thus making the latter a sort of transept to the new and longer nave. The whole structure was later fitted with a gabled roof in a nondescript style with a false "Mission" (California) parapet on the newer east façade. But the interior of the 1807 section remains the same, even to the earthen floor and the "secular period" *retablo* against the north wall.

According to Prince, Governor Mariano Martínez, the last Governor sent from Mexico in the brief period that New Mexico was under Mexican rule, planned to have a shaded park around the Rosario chapel, with a tree-lined avenue

64. AASF. See Note 41.

leading to it from the town, ostensibly to make the annual processions more beautiful. He had trees planted, and a special acequia dug to the area for watering these trees. But rapid changes in politics ended this laudable project. The native Governor who succeeded Martínez was more interested in his own affairs, besides being distracted by rumors of an American invasion, which came soon after to distract the inhabitants still more. "Perhaps before many moons, some public-spirited citizen or patriotic city council . . . may . . . make the dreary waste . . . a place of beauty and joy forever." Prince wrote this in 1913.[65]

---

65. *Op. cit.*, p. 116.

CHAPTER IV

FIESTAS AND PROCESSIONS

The Lady festivals mentioned in the earliest *Conquistadora* fragments were four in number, according to Fr. Espínola.[66] Fr. Diego de Chabarría in 1689 names two of these, the Immaculate Conception (December 8) and the Purification or Candlemas (February 2).[67] Since it is known that two of the four feasts were celebrated in December, probably the third was that of Our Lady of Guadalupe on December 12. The fourth feast may well have been that held on the first Sunday of October which, since the year 1571, had been designated by Pope St. Pius V as the annual festival of the Holy Rosary. This last is again emphasized as the principal feast of the Confraternity in its 1770 phase. Fr. Domínguez names the patronal feast of St. Francis on October 4, with Vespers and Mass, and the feast of the Holy Rosary, also with Vespers and Mass.[68] Other Marian feasts were solemnly observed, but not necessarily by the Confraternity as such. The week-day Masses often mentioned in the early fragments were not feasts, properly speaking, but regular days in which Masses were offered throughout the year for members of the Confraternity, over and above a stated number offered for each deceased member following his death.

As to Processions, just as a Confraternity revolved around a specific image of its celestial Patron, so each solemn festival was unfailingly observed with a High Mass, Vespers on the eve, and a Procession after the Mass and very often after the Vespers also. But how or when the present so-called "de Vargas Procession" began is impossible to say; by this I mean the procession with the statue from the *Conquistadora* Chapel in the Parroquia to the Rosario Chapel outside the town, and the return procession nine days later. There is no mention of such an observance in any of the old

---

66. Accounts, f. 20.
67. *Ibid.*, f. 20v.
68. *Op. cit.*, f. 4125.

Confraternity sources found so far, nor do Domínguez or Candelaria make any such reference in their descriptions of the solemnities observed on the first Sunday of October. Father Hozio, in his petition for the new chapel, echoes the people's belief that the statue rested at the Rosario site at the time of the armed reconquest of Santa Fe, and so suggests the possibility that the processions to and from the Parroquia were already taking place prior to 1806, the faithful erecting a shrine of boughs every year, as Mr. Sena recalls, which in turn suggested to them the need of a permanent structure. Certain it is that since that time the two processions have been held without interruption, with the novena of Masses at the Rosario chapel prior to the return of the statue to the Parroquia.

The reason for holding this double procession in summer is a mystery, since none of the four seventeenth-century feasts occurred in early summer; in descriptions extant of the 1770 phase of the Confraternity, nothing is said about this matter either; not until 1887, when Father deFouri wrote, do we have a definite statement that the first procession left the Cathedral on the Sunday after the Octave of Corpus Christi, and that the return procession left the Rosario chapel after nine Masses were sung there on consecutive days for a full novena.[69] However, there is no reason to doubt that these processions had been observed at such a time and in the same manner since the beginning of the last century, either before or after the erection of the Rosario Chapel.

In his newspaper article on the "De Vargas Procession," Mr. Sena describes these processions in days gone by. The first one started from the Cathedral, after Mass in the morning, straight down San Francisco Street, then over to Rosario Street, and to the chapel outside the town. *Descansos*, or shrines of rest, were erected at various stages: the first one at the home of Doña Anamaría Ortiz, where the present St. Francis School now stands (property recently acquired by the La Fonda Hotel) ; the next stop was in

69. *Op. cit.*, p. 15.

front of the *Castrense*, later the house of Felipito Delgado, and in more modern times the Capital Restaurant and Mayflower Cafe; next the home of Don Gaspar Ortiz y Alarid, the corner now occupied by the Santa Fe Book and Stationery Store; then the house of Felipe Delgado on the side of the present Lensic Theater; after this the procession halted at the home of Doña Guadalupe Miera at the intersection of San Francisco and Rosario; and the last stop, before the Rosario chapel was reached, was at the house of Don Ambrosio Ortiz at the foot of the present Johnson Street. At each shrine the priest incensed the statue and chanted a prayer. Large arches spanned the streets at various intervals, and both sides of the route were lined with evergreens stuck in the ground. The statue was returned just as solemnly by the same route at the end of a full novena which ended on Tuesday, and at six or seven o'clock in the morning. The current practice is to hold the return procession on the following Sunday, both processions being held in the afternoon, although another Mass is sung at the Rosario chapel on the next day. All old photographs of church processions on San Francisco Street and the Plaza show this "de Vargas Procession." The annual Corpus Christi procession always took a different direction, around the block on which the Cathedral, hospital, and Archbishop's residence are now located, until very recent years.

In his article, "The Virgin of the Reconquest," Dr. Espinosa shows how this double procession and its novena of Masses parallels a similar tradition in Mexico City. There Cortés also conquered with the aid of a "Lady," and he dedicated a chapel in her honor. The Cortés statue was carried every year from the Cathedral of Mexico to that chapel outside the city, and it was said that it grew heavier on the return journey, as if the Lady were reluctant to leave her own little chapel. This last bit of legend was also current in Santa Fe. Because of these exact similarities, and since de Vargas used only these two titles of *Remedios* and *Conquista*, the author concluded that no *Conquistadora* statue existed during the Reconquest of New Mexico (only the royal standard), or that, if it did exist, it acquired the title of *Rosario* in relatively modern times.

But now we know that the devotion of *Nuestra Señora del Rosario La Conquistadora* did exist in New Mexico, long before the de Vargas Reconquests of 1692 and 1693, and continued after the Reconquest, with one interruption and in two separate phases, until the present day. What, then, about the uncanny similarities between the Santa Fe and Mexico City traditions? The only answer is that the Santa Fe devotees, made aware of a similar *Conquistadora* down there, probably at the beginning of the nineteenth century when traffic and interchange of personnel became more common, took over the idea that de Vargas conquered Santa Fe as Cortés had conquered Mexico, adopting the practice of a double procession and a novena of Masses, which in turn inspired the erection of the Rosario chapel in 1807. As we have seen, all the old *Conquistadora* documents extant speak of one chapel only, the north chapel of the Parroquia, and the only major celebrations are the several Marian feasts in fall and winter without any mention of double processions to and from the Parroquia and any other chapel.

Because neither the newly-found *Conquistadora* fragments nor previously-known sources refer directly and uninterruptedly to every phase of the *Conquistadora* problem when taken singly, but rather lend their accumulated force when taken as a whole, my experience in this study has been exactly like that of a person putting together a large and complicated jig-saw puzzle. Most jagged pieces themselves gave no hint as to what they might ultimately represent, while some larger ones, or sections composed of them, provided a lead for further fitting of other pieces. Finally the general picture emerged, incomplete because many pieces are still missing, but clear enough for one to supply the missing parts and at the same time discard extraneous bits of legend.

My conclusion, then, is that the devotion and Confraternity of *Nuestra Señora del Rosario La Conquistadora* certainly existed in New Mexico in 1656-59, long before the Indian Revolt of 1680, and perhaps had its beginnings sometime after 1630 with the completion of the first permanent Parroquia, and around a statue placed there by Fr. Benavides. The Confraternity, though not the devotion itself, died out between the years 1726 and 1760, and was completely forgotten by 1770 when the people "inaugurated" a Confraternity and festival in honor of *La Conquistadora* as "newly-chosen" Patroness of the Kingdom. The devotion or cult, and the Confraternity in both its phases, revolved around the image still venerated under the same name in Santa Fe. This statue was "saved from the fury of the savages" in 1680, continued to be treasured at San Lorenzo during the 1680-1693 exile, and was returned with the colonists "enclosed in a wagon." Her first permanent chapel after the Reconquest, the new throne which de Vargas had resolved to build but which he never saw, was the north chapel of the 1717 Parroquia which continues to serve as a sidechapel to the 1886 Lamy Cathedral.

Unfortunately, the inhabitants of New Mexico had forgotten the true origin of this devotion and its famous image. The loss or destruction of the old Confraternity books in the middle of the eighteenth century, the indifference of the friars when the vigor of their Custody was curtailed at this period by the intrusion of the Diocese of Durango, and the brief emergence of the Confraternity of Our Lady of Light, all these helped to erase this and many other traditions and aspirations from popular memory. A last desperate effort to re-capture this heritage, though done blindly, was the 1770 revival of the Confraternity. The later unconscious association of the image with that of the Cortés tradition, dating from the nineteenth century, also shows this inner desire to restore and hold to something great out of the past that was fast fading away, and thus arose the parallel legends of de Vargas' vow regarding a chapel and a procession, to accommodate which the Rosario chapel was built. These nineteenth century accretions need not be decried; on the contrary, they should be encouraged and perpetuated.

What each generation, each century, contributes to a popular tradition and custom, especially when the blood coursing through the hearts of the people in each period is the same, is not only legitimate but enriching as well. Yet, the true origin of such an old tradition should not be lost sight of, however much overlaid by these later additions. How much more consoling and exhilarating it is for native New Mexicans to know that this very same charming little image in their midst united their forefathers in expressing their common social, national, and religious aspirations— not merely since the de Vargas Reconquest, as they have believed until now, but also in those sad days of the Indian Revolt and the heavy years of exile, and even as far back as those dim times three full centuries ago when their pioneer forebears were building up the "Kingdom of New Mexico and the *Villa* of the Holy Faith," of both of which *La Conquistadora* was "Patroness and Queen."

Photo by Robert Martin

*Returning from Rosario Chapel to the Cathedral, the Conquistadora
Procession passes the Art Gallery of the Museum of New Mexico*

CHAPTER V

ENGLISH TRANSLATION OF LA CONQUISTADORA FRAGMENTS*

(a) Inventory, 9 ff., ff. 3-11

f3   I, Captain Alonso del Rio, *Mayordomo*[70] of the Confraternity of Our Lady *La Conquistadora*, declare that I received everything contained of the valuables and things belonging to said Confraternity from the *Maestre de Campo* Francisco Gómez Robledo, past *Mayordomo* of said Confraternity in the year of Eighty-four; and acknowledging from memoranda and receipts which the Reverend Father Preacher Fray Francisco de Vargas, minister president of the *Real* of San Lorenzo, has presented, that eighty-four pesos of the Confraternity are due him from the said year of Eighty-four when the dues were not sufficient, during the term of said *Mayordomo* Francisco Gómez Robledo, yet in everything else I declare that I received it correctly and legally, without a single thing of value missing. Which ceremony of delivery took place before the Father Preacher Fray Francisco de Vargas, minister president of the Real of San Lorenzo, there being present together the Alférez Francisco Lucero de Godoy, Pedro Hidalgo, and the Alférez Blas Griego, secretary and deputy of said Confraternity. And that it may so appear for all time, the said Father [and] *Mayordomo* of the year Eighty-four signed it, on the twenty-sixth day of the month of February, of the year Sixteen Hundred and Eighty-five.

Fray Francisco de Vargas   Francisco Gómez Robledo   Alonso del Río
Francisco Mateo Lucero de Godoy   Before me the secretary
Pedro Hidalgo   Blas Griego

f3v   In this Real of San Lorenzo, on the Eighth day of the month of October, the year of Eighty-six, our Reverend Father Fray Pedro Gómez, President, Vice-Custos, and Ecclesiastical Judge Ordinary of these Provinces of New Mexico, audited the valuables and clothing of the Queen of the Angels[71] *La Conquistadora*, a Confraternity which is located[72] in this said *Real;* and having seen and examined all the valuables contained in the past record, his Reverend Paternity found some things unbecoming, thoroughly worn out and old, all of which he declared to be outworn; his Reverend Paternity ordered that from

---

* Archives of the Archdiocese of Santa Fe, Spanish Period, No. 1.

70. The title and office of *Mayordomo* corresponds to those of the *President* of present day societies and clubs as well as those of the *Commander* of our Veterans' organizations. For this reason the Spanish term is used throughout.

71. This Marian title is distinctly Franciscan, being that of the Mother-Church in Assisi, the *Portiuncula.* Hence the friars, and the people influenced by them, use it frequently when referring to the Virgin.

72. *Fundada.* "Founded" connotes the place of origin. The same expression is used later on at Santa Fe. See *Minutes,* f. 1v.

the clothing which could be made use of, for some vestment[73] or chasuble, that this be done, or that it be applied to some other object necessary for the adornment of the Queen of the Angels; and likewise if some valuable item or valuables could be exchanged, that this might be done, and the alms applied to other expenses of the Confraternity. Everything being cleared, of what there is today at hand, and might be of becoming use, the following inventory was made:

Images

First of all, the figure of Our Lady *La Conquistadora*, of a *vara* in height, a little more, in the round. Furthermore a Holy Christus, in the round, of a *vara* and a half in height; an Infant Jesus in the round, a little more than half a *vara;* three canvases a *vara* and a half high, one of Our Lady of Guadalupe, another of Our Father St. Francis, and the other of St. Anthony; an Infant Jesus, in the round, a thumb-to-forefinger span high;[74] an image of the *Sagrario.*[75]

Jewels

First of all a small gold pyx;[76] small stamps of tortoise-shell; four Agnus-Dei of abalone; another reliquary of St. Didacus of gilt copper; a gilt silver rose with five stones; a small filigree cross; (*Marginal note:* It was declared outworn, to be made into a nail[77] for Our Lady and a little filigree rose); three pairs of ear-rings, one pair of pearls and gold, and the other two of gilt silver with their stones, some green

---

73. *Ornamento.* A peculiarly Spanish designation for a chasuble, alone or in combination with its stole and maniple.

74. *Un xeme de alto.* This might be the tiny Infant with golden shoes which was in the Cathedral Museum. The other Infant of more than half a *vara,* just mentioned, might be the one described as holding a cross in both hands in 1697. (*Inventory,* f. 8.) There is one like it in the Cathedral Museum which is of the period and holds a long tubular cross of silver; naked and anatomically complete, it is tied to an upright stake on its small platform in order to stand erect. The present platform and stake are relatively modern.

75. *Sagrario:* A place to keep sacred vessels, a tabernacle or altar or shrine in which the Eucharist is reserved, in some great cathedrals the chapel which serves as a parish church. The use of the term here is baffling.

76. *Viril:* A glass-faced receptacle shaped like a watch or a modern lady's compact, also applied to such receptacles without any glass. If intended to hold the Sacred Host, or the golden *lunula* holding the Host, for insertion into a monstrance for exposition, it is correctly called a pyx or, with a gold half-moon clip inside for the Host, a *lunula.* The old Spanish word for the monstrance is *custodia.*

But if made to enclose relics, it is properly called a *theca* and, not quite correctly, a reliquary. The reliquary proper is shaped like a monstrance on a smaller scale, and the *theca* inserted into it as the *lunula* is inserted in the monstrance or ostensorium.

An Agnus Dei (literally, Lamb of God) was a piece of wax stamped with the figure of a lamb and blessed by the Pope; this was encased in a *viril* or *theca* for protection, and so it came to be applied also to the *theca* holding relics, especially those of unidentified martyrs of the Roman catacombs.

77. A golden pin inserted into the top of a statue's head to hold a crown secure. The *Conquistadora* statue has a hole on the top of the head, reinforced with a perforated iron clip nailed on top of the hole.

and others red; a little four-string pearl choker with a gold lamb; another of four strings of pearls, two others of brass, one of six strings with a silver cross, and the other of five with its little gold Cross and its tinsel; another little brass choker of three strings mixed with corals; another little choker of nine thick corals and gilt beads; a rosary of corals linked with little silver shells without a cross; another rosary of *peje* fishbone; a silver rose, broken.

Dresses

First of all a dress of white lamé with its gold galoon and small red fringe, lined with blue; a dress of flowered tapestry with scallops of silver and gold lined with red linen; another green dress of satin with silver scallops, lined with blue linen; another brown dress, flowered, with gold scallops, lined with red glazed linen; another dress of half lamé with blue flowers on white background, with gold scallops, lined with red glazed linen; two skirts, one of drab camlet, and the other of blue satin; four hoods, one of gold and silk of double knit with scallops of the same, and two of snakeskin, and one of netting; two other white hoods of thread crape, and small kerchief; a black skirt of ribbed silk, lined with blue linen—the blue skirt was declared outworn, and designated to be made into a drape for the cross.[78]

f.4

Mantles

First of all a blue satin mantle embroidered with gold and silver in flower-work; another of blue damask with its scallops of gold; another of greenish taffeta with its scallops of gold; two others of white satin, plain; another blue mantle of taffeta with its scallops of gold; another black mantle of silk, Sevilla-style.

Chemises

First of all seven chemises with their ruffs worked in different colors; two others of cambric, plain.

Trappings for the Palanquin[79]

First of all the trappings for the palanquin of white satin, embroidered with green; other trappings for the palanquin, black of Castilian baize.

Altar Cloths

First of all a cloth of Rouen linen, worked with blue; another cloth worked with rose; furthermore, three feather-dusters of fine plumes.

Jewels and Clothing of the Holy Christus[80]

First of all three bedsheets of Rouen linen with their scallops; a purple

---

78. *Manga:* Some sort of sleeve-like fabric shield put on crosses in those times.
79. *Las andas:* a litter, bier, or platform, for carrying images in procession.
80. This Christus, mentioned in the beginning after the Virgin, seems to have been a representation of the dead Savior in the sepulchre. This kind of figure is listed repeatedly in later inventories and could well be the one still to be seen in the north chapel. Their respective lengths, however, do not quite tally.

coverlet of lamé with flowers, lined with silver-threaded taffeta; another coverlet of white Chinese silk; five silk pillows, two embroidered and glossy with their lace-work; another pillow of Rouen linen worked with orange and blue silk; a pillowslip of yellow glazed linen.

Clothing of the Infant

First of all a rose dress with his cord and crown; two cambric shirts; f.4v *(Marginal note:* There aren't any.) another shirt of metal-twist; another shirt of netting; a dress of white fabric lined with blue taffeta; another dress of red moire [?]; another dress of green satin, with the pants [or hose] of red satin; a banner of white lamé with the cross of blue glass and silver tips; two little dresses of the Infant of St. Anthony, and three little shirts; a veil of blue taffeta with silver scallops; another of plain blue taffeta; a knitted snake of native thread; a bronze Infant a little less than half a *vara* long;[81] a trunk in which the clothing is kept; another chest, cedar, a *vara* long; another large chest, this chest was condemned because it was broken to pieces. (*Marginal note:* This chest was condemned by order of our Reverend Father Fray Pedro Gómez, Vice-Custos of this Holy Custody.)

All of which entries, just as they are specified in detail, were handed over to the *Mayordomo*, Alonso del Río; so that at all times he be bound to turn things in accordingly as contained in this book, reminding him that if he should enter something better or an addition, he must enter it in all detail at the end of this order—except ribbons or tape, since these are expendable things and can easily be lost; for although it might happen that the members, at the time it is asked of them, will give some ribbons or tape by way of dues, these may be specified at the time of accounting or delivery [of the office] by the *Mayordomo* to whomsoever succeeds him. And thanks are given him for the fine way in which he has worked, and the neatness with which he keeps the Confraternity's property. Thus his Reverend Paternity provided, ordered, and signed on said day, month and year, as above.

Fray Pedro Gómez
Vice-Custos and Ecclesiastical Judge

Before me
Fray José de Espínola
Secretary and Apostolic Notary

Additions which the *Mayordomo* of the Confraternity has made this year of Sixteen Hundred Eighty-seven. First of all, a dress of blue camlet which the *Sargento Mayor* Roque Madrid gave; a silver

---

81. The Infant of St. Anthony: there is a St. Anthony of the period in the Cathedral Museum, and the beautiful little Child is removable. But the bronze Infant must have disappeared long ago.

The "snake" mentioned between these two items could have been the banding used to lash the large standing Child to the pedestal. See note 74.

crown which Francisco Lucero de Godoy gave as dues to the Queen of the Angels when the Captain Alonso del Rio was *Mayordomo*. This book was audited in which are set down all the things belonging to the devotion and adornment of the Queen of the Angels, *La Conquistadora*, and everything is right and legal according to its entries, all kept with neatness and cleanliness, for all of which thanks are given [to the *Mayordomo*] for the care and support he has shown in everything pertaining to the Confraternity; and likewise for having made some additions which some benefactors have given during his term by way of valuables, such as dresses; and he is charged in the future not to fail in the support of said Confraternity, soliciting the usual dues, marking down clearly who gave them; and that it may so appear at all times, his Reverend Paternity signed it on the Fourteenth day of the month of April of Sixteen Hundred and Eighty-seven, in this *Real* and *Villa* of San Lorenzo, before me the undersigned notary.

Fray Nicolás López
Custos and Ecclesiastical Judge

Fray Cristóbal Daza
Apostolic Vice-Notary

On the Ninth day of June of Sixteen Hundred and Eighty-eight, Francisco Lucero de Godoy added a dress of white French figured silk, when the *Sargento Mayor* Alonso del Río was *Mayordomo*; furthermore some ear-rings of imitation pearls, and little mirrors, and a small mirror with a lead oval frame. Furthermore, another dress of green French figured silk which Francisco Lucero de Godoy gave for the bronze Infant Jesus. (*Marginal note:* This was given over to St. Michael.) [82]

This book was audited in which are set down the things and valuables belonging to Our Lady *La Conquistadora*, and it is correct and legal according to its entries [kept] with all neatness and cleanliness, for all of which thanks are given [to the *Mayordomo*] for the care and support he has shown in all that pertains to the Confra-

---

82. One of the *Conquistadora* traditions, nearly forgotten now, is that the statues of the Infant Jesus and of St. Michael went into battle together with that of the Virgin. (Espinosa, "The Virgin of the Reconquest.") And here, strange to say, these two statues are prominently mentioned more than once.

Regarding the San Miguel image, it is worthwhile touching here on a Confraternity of St. Michael which was apparently founded at the time, and for the purpose of collecting money for the project, when the San Miguel chapel was restored in 1710. All that we know of the society is found in a testimony of the expenses incurred, a document which is treated in full by George Kubler in his brochure, *The Rebuilding of San Miguel at Santa Fe in 1710* (Colorado Springs, 1939). Here also is mentioned a statue of St. Michael around which the Confraternity revolved; and it could have been this one of the Rosary Confraternity, for the same tradition treated by Espinosa in his aforementioned article also held that the St. Michael taken into battle was the one later kept in San Miguel chapel. All this makes one suspect that the *Conquistadora* statue, together with the larger Infant and San Miguel, might have gone into battle after all, even though documentary proof of this fact is still lacking.

ternity; and likewise for the additions which have been donated during his time; and he is charged that in the future he may neither fail nor falter in the support of the Confraternity, soliciting the usual dues and setting down with clarity those who give them; and that it may so appear, his Reverence signed it on the Twelfth day of the month of August of Sixteen Hundred and Eighty-eight, in this *Real* of San Lorenzo, before me the undersigned notary.

Fray Pedro Gómez
Vice-Custos and Ecclesiastical Judge

Before me
Fray Antonio de Azevedo
Apostolic Notary

f.5v I, Fray Diego de Chabarría, certify that the Confraternity of Our Lady of the Rosary spent twenty-four pesos for beeswax, all of which was used up in the festivities of Our Lady, at the expense of her *Mayordomo*, Alonso del Río; because it so appears to me I give this certification today, Wednesday, Second of February of Sixteen Hundred and Eighty-nine.

Fray Diego de Chabarría
(*The above entry crossed out with a few oblique strokes. On the margin: It does not count, erased.*)

This book was audited in which are set down the things and valuables pertaining to Our Lady, *La Conquistadora*, and it is correct and legal according to its entries, with all neatness and cleanliness, for all of which thanks are given [to the *Mayordomo*] for the care and support he has shown in everything pertaining to the Confraternity; and likewise for the additions which have been donated during his time; and he is charged in the future that he neither fail nor falter in the support of the Confraternity in collecting the dues; and because some things are no longer serviceable for the use to which they were destined, the *Mayordomo* of said Confraternity is ordered that certain skirts of Our Lady, of brown camlet lined with purple glazed linen, be declared outworn, and that some hangings be made from them for the palanquin; and a tinsel crown with gold flowers [be also condemned]; and that some ribbons be made into rosettes for the said Image of Our Lady, also applying to the palanquin some pieces of figured Rouen linen; and that some sandals of the Holy Christus be declared outworn. Thus Our Reverend Father Fray Francisco de Vargas, Preacher and Custos, and Ecclesiastical Judge Ordinary of this Holy Custody of the Conversion of St. Paul of New Mexico, provided and ordered, on the Twenty-third of May of Sixteen Hundred and Eighty-nine, before me the undersigned notary.

Fray Francisco de Vargas
Custos and Ecclesiastical Judge

Before me
Fray Agustín de Colina
Apostolic Notary

When Our Reverend Father Fray Francisco de Vargas, Preacher, Custos, and Ecclesiastical Judge Ordinary of these Provinces and Kingdom of New Mexico, was auditing the book of valuables pertaining to the Confraternity of Our Lady, *La Conquistadora*, in this *Real* of San Lorenzo, his Paternity found not a thing missing, examining its entries in this book; of course, his Paternity ordered the *Mayordomo* of said Confraternity to condemn a black satin skirt and have it made into a drape[83] for the cross; likewise, a small cross and a little filigree rose, to make from them a nail for the crown of Our Lady;[84] and the *Mayordomo* having been charged to give an account before us, together with his deputies, his Very Reverend Paternity examined the records and books in which the members are set down; and said *Mayordomo* being charged concerning the number of the members set down, and what could be seen of the dues, and his expenses of the Confraternity, we noticed that the dues of some of the members were missing; when said *Mayordomo* had presented his receipts, and among them one [point that stood out] is that many of the members of this Kingdom are absent, here he gave us a satisfactory account from his own memory, and declared what he knew at present regarding the dues, which are a hundred and forty-one pesos, paid through the Syndic[85] to the Father Preacher Fray Jose Espínola Almonacid, minister of said Convent of the *Real* of San Lorenzo, who [the latter two] declared this to be the truth. And at the request of the *Mayordomo* and the members, they petitioned his Reverend Paternity to make a new roster-book of the members; his Paternity realized from said book and petition that the making of a new book was most convenient [for] listing the members who at present are found in this Kingdom, and among these the ones who give and help with their dues each year, so that said *Mayordomo* may give his accounts in the future without anyone, who is approached with care, failing by this procedure towards the utility and welfare of the members, living and deceased, so that Justice is distributive and all partake of the divine suffrages; and because his Very Reverend Paternity recognized the labor, solicitude, and effort with which said *Mayordomo* and deputies of said Confraternity work to increase it, we give thanks for the job well done as they promise us to try hard in the future not to fail this order, both those who are at present [officers] and those who may be in the future. Thus his Reverend Paternity provided, ordered, and signed it on the Fourteenth of May of Sixteen Hundred and Ninety-one, before me the undersigned secretary and Apostolic Notary —and likewise his Reverend Paternity ordered that the old book be preserved, and he signed it on said day, month and year, as above.

Fray Francisco de Vargas
    Custos and Ecclesiastical Judge

83. See note 78.
84. See note 77.
85. *Síndico:* The layman who handled the Franciscans' finances.

Before
Fray Antonio Guerra
Secretary and Apostolic Notary

On the Thirtieth day of the Month of November of Sixteen Hundred and Ninety-one, the *Alférez* Francisco Lucero de Godoy gave as dues[86] a dress for the most holy Virgin of Chinese figured silk, or figured satin which is mostly red, with its . . . . .[*illegible*] of the same material, the *Sargento Mayor* Francisco Anaya Almazán being *Mayordomo*. Furthermore, a tunic of white embroidered gauze which a member, named Juana de Alemán, gave as dues.

f.6v

On his juridical Visit, Our Reverend Father Fray Joaquín de Hinojosa, Preacher, Vice-Custos, and Ecclesiastical Judge Ordinary of these Provinces and Kingdom of New Mexico, examined this book in which are entered the valuables of the Confraternity: and having seen that there are some things which, according to what has been decreed by the Holy Office, must not be put on Images, but rather that from the hoods and chemises some tabernacle veils[87] may be made, and that [material] from the dresses of the Infant Jesus be applied to other things of his cult; and the beads, pearls, and jewels can be given as well-applied to the shrine of the Most Blessed Sacrament, the ownership of all this always remaining with the Confraternity of Our Lady *La Conquistadora*. The hat was declared outworn; and let some rosettes be made from the plumes. And the Infant Jesus' green dress of figured satin was turned over to the image of St. Michael. And inasmuch as the *Mayordomo* and deputies of this Confraternity claimed ownership of a silver lamp which was in the Convent of Socorro, it was given to them because it belongs to the Confraternity, together with a silver vase without base—there being until now no other [claim] to the contrary. And a silver diadem was given to them in lieu of a silver crown which, they say, was lost and belongs to the Confraternity. And for better government of said Confraternity, and so that those who are remiss in their dues may not think that they participate in the suffrages without helping the Confraternity as they ought—his Reverend Paternity decreed that, when one or some of the members are remiss for three or four years successively, the *Mayordomo* must request the Father Guardian of this Convent of the Real to admonish them publicly; and if they do not amend, they will be erased from the roster of the book and may not participate in the usual suffrages; and he will request the same of the Fathers Minister of the rest of the Convents of this Kingdom. And regarding the dues in arrears: the absent representatives[88] will

---

86. *Límosna:* Alms, literally; then carried over to mean the dues required periodically of the members. Many times it is difficult or even impossible to distinguish the dues from some extra free donation.

87. *Palias:* Altar-cloths, if made of linen. Tabernacle-veils, if made of any other material, and covered with embroidery.

88. *Podatarios:* Those who have power of attorney. How these absent individuals will be reached is not clear.

be approached for their dues, and those dues which should be acquired from former years must always be noted down as such; so that in the Visitation everything is patent. And the old book, which is not in a decent condition, will be burned, after the [names of] the members have been transferred. And as to the present *Mayordomo*, the *Sargento Mayor* Cristóbal Tapia, and Deputies, many and repeated thanks are given him for the additions made and the punctuality with which he has worked; we charge him anew that he continue in his faithfulness, which the Queen of the Angels, Our Lady, will reward for the services in behalf of her devotion. Thus his Reverend Paternity provided, ordered, and signed on the First of September of this year of Sixteen Hundred and Ninety-two, before me the undersigned Secretary and Apostolic Notary.

Fray Joaquín de Hinojosa
Ecclesiastical Judge

Before me
Fray Agustín de Colina
Secretary and Apostolic Notary

f.7 A silver lamp which was brought out of New Mexico [and] which was kept at the Convent of Socorro and was returned to the Confraternity because it was its property.[89] Furthermore, a silver diadem which belonged to the Convent of el Paso, and was exchanged for a silver crown which belonged to this Confraternity.

The *Maestre de Campo* and Lieutenant General, Luis Granillo, *Mayordomo* of the Confraternity of Our Lady of the Rosary, Juan del Río, Francisco Jurado, Juan Pacheco, and Cristóbal Jaramillo, deputies, and Pedro Hidalgo, secretary, declare and certify that we received all the valuables accordingly as are contained in the record of this book, except: what the preceding *auto* of our Reverend Father Vice-Custos, Fray Joaquín de Hinojosa, declared as outworn in the Visitation, and that it may so appear we signed it, of those who know how to sign, on the Twenty-third of the Month of May of Sixteen Hundred and Ninety-three.

Luis Granillo
Juan Pacheco
Juan del Río
Pedro Hidalgo
Secretary

Additions which the Lieutenant General of this Kingdom, Luis Granillo, has made from the years Ninety-two and three, until that of Ninety-five, during which there was elected as *Mayordomo* the Lord Governor and Captain-General Don Diego de Vargas Zapata Luján Ponce de León, and as his assistant *Mayordomo*, the aforesaid Lieutenant General, Luis Granillo.

First of all a vestment of Chinese damask, yellow and white, which

---

89. One reference which points to the existence of the Confraternity before the Indian revolt.

consists of a chasuble, stole, maniple, frontal, chalice pall, and burse for corporals; said vestment proceeding from some East Indian goods which the Lord Governor gave as dues. (*Marginal notes:* Further, three pesos were spent in providing said vestment. Further, six *varas* of thin sash that serve the Lady, which are worth three pesos.—A large box with its lock and a small box inside.) Further, six brass candlesticks; a tin-sheet lantern, large, and [with] glass windows; an iron rod two *varas* long for Our Lady's curtain; a large canopy of double taffeta, red and yellow, which serves as a throne-canopy which the Lord Governor gave as dues. Furthermore he left sixteen wax candles.

f.7v

Additions of the year 95

First of all, two silver candlesticks which the Lord Governor, *Mayordomo* of the Confraternity, gave. A dress of blue, flowered silk brocade lined with red taffeta; four *varas* and a half of red silk ribbon two fingers wide, all for said dress; a camlet chemise with lace; a seat-covering [?] of silk, white, green, and yellow.

I, Captain Antonio Montoya, assistant *Mayordomo*, declare, to-together with the deputies and secretary, that I received of the Lieutenant General Luis Granillo all the valuables accordingly as they are set down in this book, and that it may so appear we signed it on the Fifteenth of April of this Year of Sixteen Hundred and Ninety-three.

Antonio de Montoya   Before me
Luis Martín   Antonio Lucero de Godoy
Sebastián Gonzales   Secretary of said Confraternity

f.8 I, the Captain Don Alonso, declare that, as assistant *Mayordomo* of the Mother of God, I received from the Captain, Antonio Montoya, the following valuables:

First of all, Our Lady *La Conquistadora* with dress, mantle,[91] silver crown, an Agnus-Dei, a theca, and a Rosary; furthermore, the Child Jesus with a Cross in its hands and a silvered band and base;[92] another Child of bronze; a "Jesus the Nazarene" on canvas; Our Lady of the *Sagrario* on canvas; Our Lady of Solitude on canvas; Our Lady of *Remedios* painted on elkskin; Our Lady of the Rosary on the guidon;[93] another Child Jesus of wood; a silver lamp; a glass lantern;

---

91. *Ornamento* is used here, perhaps because it looked like a chasuble to this layman's eye.
92. *Supeana:* (Latin: *supedaneum.*) The platform before an altar, or a platform-like pedestal for a statue. This one is mentioned in connection with a silvered *band* of the Child Jesus, which is significant. See notes 74 and 81.
93. Three of these Madonna paintings are intriguing: 1) Our Lady of the *Sagrario*, because of its puzzling name; 2) Our Lady of *Remedios* on elkskin, because it brings to mind a large charming painting of the Virgin with a giant Rosary and the legend: *Ymagen Milagrosa de Nuestra Señora de Begoña, 1608.* It is in the

f.8v   Furthermore, six candlesticks, four small and two large; eleven bronze candlesticks (*Marginal note:* The small ones belong to the church, and only two to the Confraternity); eight dresses which with the one the Virgin has on, are nine. Likewise I received all the clothing that belongs to the most holy Virgin, and that it may so appear I sign it with the deputies on the Third of February of the Year of 1697.

> Alfonso Rael de Aguilar
> Antonio Montoya
> At the request of Sebastián
> Gonzáles
> José de Contreras
> At the request of Luis Martín
> José de Contreras

f.9   I, Sebastián Gonzáles, assistant *Mayordomo*, declare that I received on the Third Day of March of 1698, from the hand of the Captain Don Alonso Rael de Aguilar, the following valuables which are the property of the Confraternity of Our Lady of the Rosary.

The Lord Governor and Captain-General Don Pedro Rodríguez de Cubero[94] gave as an addition the following: an imperial gold-plated silver crown, inlaid and garnished with stones. Further, a dress of red brocade with its blue mantle of the same.

The Lord General Don Diego de Vargas gave a blue figured-silk dress and white mantle; and a white frontal of gold-lace, and a chasuble of the same.

The *Mayordomo*, Sebastián Gonzales, added some altar-cloths, a tabernacle-veil figured with silk, and twelve candlesticks.

Auto of Visitation. In the Villa of Santa Fe, on May Thirtieth of Seventeen Hundred and Two, Our Reverend Father Fray Antonio Guerra, Preacher, Custos of the Holy Custody of the Conversion of St. Paul, and Ecclesiastical Judge Ordinary by Apostolic Authority of this Kingdom and Provinces of New Mexico, etc., in making his juridical Visitation, his Reverend Paternity ordered Sebastián Gonzales Bernal, assistant *Mayordomo*, to appear in order to give the accounts of the dues which the Confraternity of Our Lady *La Conquistadora* has received. Who appeared before his Reverend Paternity with the books of said Confraternity and, when his entries had been examined,

---

Galisteo church, a successor of the post-Reconquest Galisteo Mission of Our Lady of *Remedios*; 3) Our Lady of the Rosary *on the guidon* or banner. See note 40. Perhaps, too, Aguilar, a layman and a soldier, switched the names around, so that the Lady on the guidon is *Remedios* and the one on elkskin is mistakenly called "the Rosary." This bears looking into because Antonio José Ortiz' home-chapel in Santa Fe was used as parish church while he was rebuilding and enlarging the Parroquia after 1798, and his immediate descendants had much to do with the Galisteo churches.

94. Cubero, de Vargas' successor as Governor, also took over as *Mayordomo* of the Confraternity. Could it be that the *Reconquistador*, mentioned right after, sent his gift from his jail-cell in Santa Fe?

it was discovered that nine years[95] had passed without the accounts being kept, for which reason they were full of confusion and almost impossible to adjust. Wherefore his Reverend Paternity ordered that henceforth the *Mayordomo* must make a book in which he shall set down with all clarity and exactness whatever he should receive as dues, and their distribution and expenditure.

f.9v   And every four months he must come with said book to this Convent of said Villa and, together with the Father Guardian of it (to whom his Reverend Paternity grants his authority for this purpose) let the accounts be adjusted, and signed by both, so that at the end of the year, when the election of the *Mayordomo* is held, they may be made public to the members, and it may be seen how their dues have been employed in the Masses, feasts, and functions of Our Lady, and in some additions; and this will serve them as a solace, and the faithful will be encouraged to have themselves inscribed in this holy brotherhood; and likewise with this diligence the Prelate on his Visitation will have less work to go through; and should, he discover some omission on the part of the *Mayordomo* and deputies, they shall be debarred from exercising said offices; and those who should work faithfully the Divine Majesty of God our Lord will reward them with spiritual gifts, favoring them as servants of the Queen of the Angels. Thus his Reverend Paternity provided, ordered, and signed on said day, month and year, as above, before me the undersigned notary.

Fray Antonio Guerra
Custos and Ecclesiastical Judge
Before me
Fray Miguel Muñiz
Apostolic Notary

f.10   In the Villa of Santa Fe, on the First Day of the Month of May of Seventeen Hundred and Four, I, the Captain Juan Páez Hurtado,[96] Lieutenant General and Captain-General of this Kingdom of New Mexico, as *Mayordomo* of the Confraternity of Our Lady *La Conquistadora*, received from Sebastián Gonzales all the valuables belonging to the Confraternity, the tenor of which is as follows:

First of all, a new red dress of silk with gold flowers, embellished with a fine French galoon matching the flowers of the silk fabric, with a mantle of gold-flowered blue silk with the same embellishment; another dress of blue gold-flowered Florentine silk, much worn out, without mantle; another dress of Florentine silk with red, green, and blue flowers, worn-out, and without mantle; another dress of white lamé, old, with a mantle of white gold-flowered silk embellished with an imitation gold galloon a finger wide; another dress of brown silk

---

95. Since 1693, the year of the Reconquest and the return of the colonists.
96. He succeeded de Vargas as acting Governor in April, 1704; on May 1 he took over as *Mayordomo* of the Confraternity—and three days later he entered his petition to marry Doña Teodora García de la Riva. Years later, both came to rest in the *Conquistadora* chapel.

with white flowers, embellished with imitation buttons which serve as a border, old, and without mantle; another white dress of old tapestry embellished with gold-point lace, without mantle; another dress of green tapestry without embellishment and mantle, much worn **f.10** out; another dress of blue camlet with old blue embroidered mantle; a gilt silver crown with 25 imitation stones, green, blue, and red, with its surmounting cross; another old, plain, silver crown; some altarcloths of Rouen linen five *varas* long; three bedsheets, two of Morlaix linen and one of Rouen, with Lorraine lace; a quilt of purple Chinese lamé, embellished with a wide lace of native thread, lined with greenish taffeta; a cushion of black plain taffeta and another of said taffeta; a corpse-kerchief[97] of Brittany linen with fine point lace; an old gilt Agnus-Dei of silver with relics of different saints; a little gold deer [?] with an uneven pearl; a gilt silver rose with five stones, and the said stones imitation, white, blue, and green; some Chamberg-style earrings of gilt silver filigree with two blue imitation stones and two crystal globules, and each ear-ring with two pendants of four fine pearls each; some other ear-rings of gilt silver filigree, each with a crystal amulet; a gold reliquary inlaid with blue, with four little pillars at **f.11** the corners; a coral rosary with seven mysteries on a silver chain; another rosary of mermaid-bone [sea-cow] with seven mysteries[98]; three dresses for the Child,[99] one purple, another red, and another white, all old; all of which aforesaid valuables I have received, as has been said, and that it may so appear, I signed it on said day as above.

Juan Páez Hurtado

Likewise, a tabernacle-veil of green puffed [?] silk moire [?] which the wife of the negro drummer[100] gave to Our Lady *La Conquistadora;* a skirt of green camlet which Micaela de Velasco gave to Our Lady, and which is worn beneath the dress.

[F. 11v *is blank.*]

(b) Accounts, I f., f.20

f.20 I, Fray Francisco de Vargas, state that I have received from the *Mayordomo,* Alonso del Río, as well as from the deputies, the

---

97. See note 80.

98. A mystery, also called a "decade," consists of one *Paternoster* and ten *Avemarias.* The common "Dominican" rosary is composed of five mysteries, on which are prayed the three sets of Joyful, Sorrowful, and Glorious Mysteries (or incidents) in the life of Christ and His Mother. But this twice-mentioned rosary has seven decades or mysteries, and therefore is the Franciscan Rosary composed of one set of Seven Joyous Mysteries only. Very likely this was the one prayed exclusively by the New Mexicans in those days.

99. This seems to be *the* Child of the *Conquistadora.*

100. Sebastián Rodríguez, drummer, widower of Isabel Olguín, and son of Manuel Rodríguez and María Fernández, both Negroes of Luanda, in Guinea, married Juana de la Cruz, *coyota,* of unknown parents, May 12, 1697. In 1707 he deeded some land in Santa Fe south of the river to Micaela de Velasco, the donor mentioned in the same paragraph.

dues consisting of one hundred and three pesos and four *tomines*, on the account of the Confraternity of Our Lady *La Conquistadora*, which dues are applied in the Holy Sacrifice of the Mass for the benefit of the souls of the members of the Confraternity, both living and dead: especially the said dues which said Alonso del Río finished collecting, which was to pay eighty-four pesos which the Confraternity owed in the time of the preceding *Mayordomo*, Francisco Gómez Robledo, who found the alms insufficient because the members were in dire need and not all could give, and so the present *Mayordomo*, having carried out his duties punctually, finished collecting said dues, and without owing me anything since the time that he has had the Confraternity under his care. Moreover, I do know from experience that he does it with charity, zeal, and solicitude, along with the deputies who accompany him, each one of whom takes pains to excel in the service of the Most Serene Queen of Heaven, Most Holy Mary. And that this my receipt will always so appear, I signed it on the Eighth day[101] of the Month of May, Sixteen Hundred and Eighty-five.

Fray Francisco de Vargas

I, Fray José de Espínola, Father and minister president of this *Real* of San Lorenzo, state that I have received from Captain Alonso del Río, *Mayordomo* of the Confraternity of the Queen of the Angels, *La Conquistadora*, one hundred and sixty-three pesos since the Seventh of June for the Masses of the members living and deceased, and likewise of the four festivities of the Queen of the Angels, and so that this may so appear at all times, I gave this along with a receipt in duplicate of the Reverend Father Fray Juan Muñoz of the time when he said the Masses, and in confirmation I signed it on the Second day of the month of February of this current year of Eighty-six.

f.20v

Fray José de Espínola

I, Fray Diego de Chabarría, Preacher and Father Minister president of this *Real* of San Lorenzo, state that I have received from Captain Alonso del Río,[102] *Mayordomo* of the Confraternity of Our Lady of the Rosary *La Conquistadora*, eighty pesos since the Thirteenth of October for Masses for members of the Confraternity, living and deceased, as well as for two feasts which were celebrated in honor of Our Lady, the one of the Conception, the other of the Purification, and that this may so appear at all time I gave a receipt on the Second day of the month of February of Eighty-nine.

Fray Diego de Chabarría

---

101. A hole was already punched in the paper when Fr. de Vargas wrote on it, so that the word *días* in the next line curves down to avoid it. Four years after, Fr. Chabarría wrote the last three letters of *Rosario* on the punched flap adhering to the reverse side of the sheet.

102. Captain Alonso del Río lost everything in the Pueblo Revolt. He did not return to New Mexico in 1693, but remained stationed at the el Paso presidio, and was considered an "old-timer" there in 1709. Undoubtedly he was one of the members who kept sending up their dues to Santa Fe long after the Reconquest.

(c) Accounts, "Cuaderno Segundo," 1 f.

f.1 Second Volume in twenty-two leaves.

1689

Book in which are set down the dues which the Confraternity of Our Lady *La Conquistadora* has in receipt: this book is made up of twenty leaves; this book begins today, Fourteenth of June of Sixteen Hundred and Eighty-six.

Receipt of the Dues of the Confraternity

First of all, the Lord Governor and Captain-General Don Domingo de Jironza[103] gave as dues three wax candles worth three pesos; our Very Reverend Father Custos, Fray Francisco de Vargas, gave some socks worth one peso; the General gave two pesos' worth of soap; Diego Arias one peso's worth of soap; the *Sargento Mayor* Francisco de Anaya, *Mayordomo* of the Queen of the Angels, gave as dues, for himself and his wife, two pairs of socks worth two pesos; Doña Jacinta de Quirós some understockings worth one peso; Inez de Tapia gave as dues one peso's worth of soap; Josefa Barba gave one peso's worth of soap; Francisco Romero de Pedraza gave as dues for himself and for his wife one *campeche* [wood, honey, wax?] worth four pesos, two for this year and two for last year; the Captain Pedro de Sedillo gave as dues a sheep worth one peso; Cristóbal Tapia some understockings worth one peso; Juana de Valencia, his wife, gave some socks worth one peso; Pablo *"el viejo"* four chickens worth one peso; Doña Lucía Barela de Losada gave as dues two yards of red ribbon; Angelina paid f.1v two pairs of fine socks worth four pesos; the Adjutant Antonio Lucero paid some bracelets of black bead-work and synthetic pearls worth two pesos, for himself and for his wife; Pedro de Leyba for himself and for his wife paid, from the dues, some white woolen socks and some black and white understockings, [what a woolly guy?]: they are worth two pesos; the Father Commissary, Fray Juan Muñoz, paid as his dues a wax candle worth one peso; our Father Fray Diego de Mendoza paid his dues with one wax candle worth one peso; Juan Olguín paid his dues with four chickens worth one peso; Francisco Frésquez paid his dues for himself and for his wife with one sheep and one ewe a year old, each head worth one peso, they are two pesos; Mateo Lucas, Governor of Ysleta[104] paid his dues with a year-old sheep, value of one peso; the Father Fray Antonio de Azevedo paid his dues with a wax candle, value of one peso; Ambrosio Frésquez paid his dues with some small shoes valued at two pesos, for himself and for his wife; Juan García paid, for himself and for his wife, his dues for this pres-

103. Don Domingo Jironza de Cruzate. Neither he nor his immediate predecessors were *Mayordomos*, which makes one suspect that de Vargas had himself elected to this pious office.
104. Not the New Mexico Pueblo, but one of the 1680 settlements in the el Paso district.

ent year and the past year of Eighty-eight, two *varas* of Brittany linen, value of four pesos; Diego de Luna paid his dues with a pound of chocolate worth two pesos, for himself and for his wife—

(d) Accounts, 4 ff., f.1-f.4

f.1 I paid the Reverend Father Fray Lucas de Arébalo 6 pesos' worth on account of the Monday Masses, with a spade; further I paid the Reverend Father Fray Juan Mingues 4 pesos for the Masses of the Captain Juan de Dios Lucero de Godoy; further, the Reverend Father Fray Lucas took two buckskins for the Monday Masses of the Confraternity, and a sheaf of tobacco; received from Fray Lucas 6 pesos; received from Captain Montoya of Bernalillo three sheep, and three from Juan Gonzales. which the Father Guardian received; received for the dues of the members of Our Lady in El Paso 13 pesos through Antonio Tafoya; on August 13 I received from the deputies of the Most Illustrious Confraternity of Our Lady of the Rosary thirty pesos which they collected on said day; likewise I received a wax candle worth one peso; likewise I received two pesos' value in some shoes; likewise I received four sheep; on September 4 I received from the deputy, Diego Marquez, four pesos; on said day I received from Captain Vargas[105] four pesos; further, three pesos from "la Mosonga" and from Bartolo "the little chanter"; on September 4 I received two pesos; on September 10 I received five pesos; on the 11th, three pesos; on the 15th I received two pesos from Juan de León; on the 24th I received four pesos; on the 26th I received two pesos; on October 2, I received two **f.1v** pesos; on the 18th I received two pesos; on the 22nd I received two pesos; on the 28th I received from Captain Roybal[106] three thin elkskins and a thick one, two bison hides, two pairs of shoes, and a peso's worth; on the 29th I received two pesos; further I received 4 pesos from Captain Diego Montoya; on November 3 I received two pesos; on December 9 I received some shoes; on the same day, a buckskin; on the 12th of said [month] some shoes; on the 13th I received eleven bushels of wheat from La Cañada; likewise I received six pesos from a bushel of horse-beans and peas which my *compadre*, the Barber,[107] received and which he will make good at the Palace; further,

---

105. Not the Governor, of course. There were people of this name living in New Mexico before and after the Reconquest. Capt. Sebastián Vargas and Maria de Leyba, his wife, were marriage witnesses in Santa Fé, August 13, 1730.

Juana de la Cruz, "alias Mosonga," died May 9, 1727, the wife of Juan de Ledesma.

106. Ignacio de Roybal y Torrado was born near Santiago de Compostela, in Galicia, joined the Reconquest army as a 21-year old soldier, and married Francisca Gómez Robledo six weeks after the battle for Santa Fe. He received a large grant near San Ildefonso and by 1696 was the officer in charge of that military jurisdiction. One of his many sons, Santiago, became the first native priest in New Mexico, a secular, who later became Vicar General and was closely connected with the Confraternity of Our Lady of Light. Other children and grandchildren appear in the Rosario Confraternity records in both its phases.

107. Antonio Durán de Armijo, native of Zacatecas, "*de oficio barbero*," married

two pesos from Antonia de Manzanares; I further received two bushels of wheat from Nicolás Griego for the widow Archuleta which I took from the freight of my cart. [*This entry crossed out.*] On January 22 I received two pesos; on February 3 I received three pesos; on March 28 of 1714 I received four pesos; further, I received a small Apache girl[108] whom I sold for 67 pesos to pay the Reverend Father Guardian for the Masses and fiestas of the Confraternity; likewise I received last year of 1713, from the dues of the soldier-members, sixty-five pesos, which I paid to the Lord Governor in the amount of a hundred and twenty-two, in that the *Marqués* de la Peñuela[109] left it as a loan the time that he was *Mayordomo;* likewise I received this year of 1714

f.2 from the dues of the soldier-members, with some that were entered anew, a hundred and six pesos, and from them I paid the Lord Governor fifty-seven, with which I finished paying the hundred and twenty-two of the *Marqués,* and the Confraternity existing in the *Palacio* has forty-nine pesos today, March 17, 1714; further, I received eleven pesos in soap from el Paso; further, two candles at 6 a pound; further I received six sheep from Albuquerque; further, I received from Baltasar Trujillo, from the dues of el Paso, fifteen pesos of monkscloth which I made good [sold?] at the Palace; further I made good eleven pesos at the Palace, and six which my wife took in a pair of shoes and a yard of linen, which amount to 32 with the above entry; further, I received from the Reverend Father Guardian, Fray Antonio Carmago, eight pesos' value in four sheep from the dues of Albuquerque; I gave to the Reverend Father Fray José Guerrero eleven pesos' worth of Brittany linen from the dues of el Paso; I received a peso's

---

María de Quirós in 1695. He was still called *"el Maestro Barbero"* when he died, June 22, 1753.

108. The enslavement and sale of one's fellowman is repugnant to us who are the inheritors of a painfully slow social development. But Christianity as a whole, composed of human beings with clouded minds, has taken centuries to *realize* the import of cardinal principles left by its Founder. For example, not many decades ago men in civilized countries were jailed for debt, and it is only in our time that men began to realize the basic Christian justice of a living wage, which many still refuse to see.

At this period other nationalities and the strictest Protestant sects accepted and practiced slavery as a matter of course. But the Spaniards, as in this case, made slaves from wild tribes only, and with this marked difference from, say, the English practice. The slaves were treated as minor members of the family and instructed in the Faith, with prospects of freedom as soon as they were civilized. They could marry, and their children were born free according to law. As an example, there is the case of Regina Roybal, a nomadic Indian captive who was given her master's family name. In 1752 a Frenchman by the name of Juan Mifión (Mignon) asked for her hand and they were married. Since their children left no male issue, the name has not survived. The case of the Negro drummer (see note 100) is another instance of the eventual adoption into the community of the savage or his children through this then necessary process of servitude.

109. Don José Chacón Medina Salazar y Villaseñor, the Governor who on September 16, 1712, issued an edict for a perpetual celebration with a Fiesta of the 1692 Conquest. Evidently he took over the presidency of the Confraternity together with the Governorship.

worth of soap; I received thirty-two pesos from the dues of Our Lady, from those who are at the Palace; I received from the members of San Buenaventura[110] nine head of cattle, which I have let go for fourteen pesos, besides another beef from San Buenaventura which the friar killed on the way. As for the rest, my *compadre* Juan García knows who owes them; further, I received from Miguel de la Cruz four pesos—

f.2v On the 1st of February of 1715 I received the dues of La Cañada,[111] three bushels of wheat; eight sacks and a half of maize; some cotton-thread understockings worth 3 pesos, and two pairs of gloves; two pesos' worth of little tomatoes—which I took, and owe the Confraternity; I received forty-one pesos on March 17, 1715, of the dues of the *Villa;* I received four pesos from Rosa Jirón; I received from Salvador de Archuleta three pesos' worth of soap, and from Tomás Núñez four pesos' worth of soap, and two sheaves and a half of tobacco; I received four pesos of the dues from the widow [?] of "el Xeco" [?] and his mother-in-law; I received two pesos' worth of little tomatoes from Andrés de Archuleta [crossed out]; I received ten pesos from my *compadre* the Barber in soap and tobacco; I received a sheaf of tobacco from Mateo Trujillo; I received another from Montes de Oca; I received three pesos from Antonio Montoya, Jr.; I received as the dues of el Paso forty-one pesos in wax at four pesos a pound; on the 1st of May of 1715 I received four pesos' worth of soap; further, 3 pesos from Juan de Rivera of Pojoaque; I received from Captain Juan Gonzales of the dues from the Río Abajo three sheep and a ewe, three small buckskins at a peso each, the two, and one at two pesos, four pairs of stockings, and one of gloves; I received seventeen pesos of dues from La Villanueva in elkskins and pieces of cloth;

f.3 Further, I received from the dues of Bernalillo two pairs of gloves worth 2 pesos; likewise, I have to charge about five hundred and fifty pesos from last year of 1715 and 1716, including in said dues 100 pesos from an Apache woman who was raffled,[112] for their having given her to Our Lady, and regarding these I have written to Mexico inquiring about a side-altar [or reredos ?] for the greater adornment of the Lady; likewise, I received from the Father Fray Miguel Muñoz, deputy from the Río Abajo, six pesos of the Confraternity; I received four pesos from the dues of La Cañada; on June 6 I received eight pesos from the dues of the members of Alburquerque; on the 8th I received four pesos' value in a canopy and some shoes from the dues of Albur-querque; I received five sheep from the dues of Alburquerque and Ber-

110. Mission San Buenaventura de Cochití, under whose spiritual administration were the Spanish settlement of La Cañada de Cochití and some of the *"ranchos de la Peña Blanca."*

111. *La Villanueva de la Cañada de la Santa Cruz,* re-settled by de Vargas as a "new Villa" with the families of *"Españoles Mexicanos"* sent up by the Viceroy in 1693.

112. See note 108.

nalillo; I received two pesos from Salvador de Archuleta; I received from the Father Fray Miguel a buckskin, and some gloves from the dues of Bernalillo; I received a sheep from the Father Fray Miguel; I received 28 pesos' worth from 7 bushels of wheat from La Cañada; I received 16 pesos' worth in four bushels of wheat from La Cañada; I received a string of chile worth 2 pesos; I received four pesos from **f.3v** Bernardo de Sena; likewise, I received seventy-five pesos from the dues of el Paso through Baltasar Trujillo; likewise eleven pesos more from the dues of La Cañada.

On the Third day of the Month of October of Seventeen Hundred and Seventeen, I, Bernardo de Sena, went in as *Mayordomo* of the Confraternity of Our Lady of the Rosary, and have received the following— I received from the Deputy of La Cañada, Tomás Núñez, sixty-four pesos which were collected from the brethren of Our Lady in wheat and chile; on the 10th of October I went out with the deputies to collect the dues in this *Villa* of Santa Fe, and a hundred and seventeen pesos were collected; I collected twenty pesos more in this *Villa;* I received from the deputy of el Paso, the sergeant Cristóbal Trujillo, seventeen pesos in wax for the use of the Confraternity; further, two pesos which they paid in two *varas* of Toledo cloth; I received seven pesos in monkscloth, which I gave to the Father Guardian; all receipts accounted for, they amounted to five hundred eleven pesos. Further I received from the Captain Juan Gonzales forty sheep which Our Lady has in the year 1718; further, 10 more old sheep in said year.

Beginning in the year 1719, I, the said *Mayordomo*, received the following: On October 19 of last year, 1718, I received from the deputy of La Cañada, Tomás Núñez, 120 pesos in wheat and chile; I collected and received in the *Villa* of Santa Fé sixty-nine pesos; I received at the Palace in account of the soldier-gentlemen 75 pesos in 25 pounds of beeswax; I further collected eight pesos more in four strings of chile; further, three pesos' worth of ribbon which I received, which was used up to make roses for Our Lady.

f.4 Further, three pesos which I gave to the Reverend Father Guardian; another four which I received and spent on paper to make a book [of accounts] for Our Lady; I received seven pesos in wax from the deputy of el Paso, Cristóbal Trujillo; I received from the deputy of the Río Abajo, on the 17th day of May, 1719, 40 pesos' value in rams and stockings and goats. Further I received 2 pesos' worth in eggs; I received at the Palace the hundred and thirty-eight pesos which the canopy cost; I collected in the *Villa* of Santa Fé nineteen pesos in wax; I received another sixteen pesos which I collected in said *Villa;* I received in said *Villa* a hundred and three pesos which I collected from the members of said *Villa;* I received seven pesos from the deputy Juan Gonzales; I received in account of the Lord Governor, Don Antonio Valverde,[113] in La Cañada, a hundred and six pesos; I collected fifty-

---

113. Antonio Valverde y Cosío succeeded Hurtado, acting Governor and also *Mayordomo* in 1717, as interim Governor and here, evidently, as *Mayordomo* as well.

two pesos in the *Villa* which I turned over to the Lord Governor; I turned over to the Lord Governor sixty-four pesos which I made from the old sheep and the wool which I received; I received in this *Villa* three bushels of wheat which I turned over to José Antonio Fernández on the account of the Lord Governor, and one was left; I received eight pesos from the deputy Gonzales; I received on account of the Lord Governor ten pounds of wax, which were used up on the Day of the Purification of Our Lady: it amounts to thirty pesos;

f.4v   I received an *arroba*[114] and a half of wax for the year's use, which the Lord Governor gave to me. It brought in a hundred and thirteen pesos and four *reales*; I received from the Lord Governor five *varas* of Rouen linen which were placed on the windows of the Chapel of Our Lady, and a length of ribbon, all of which amounted to twelve pesos; I received a flagon of wine which the Lord Governor gave me for the Saturday and Monday Masses: it was worth ten pesos; further, eight pounds of wax which the Lord Governor gave me, which are worth twenty-four pesos; further, I spent eighteen pesos for three deceased brethren, for whom Masses were said, as will appear from the bills; I received ten rams which I took from the fifty that I removed from the flock of Our Lady, and which I turned over to the Father Guardian, Fray Francisco de Yrazábal, and the forty which I received I turned over to Corís, which was on the Lord Governor's account, and twenty sheep which I received from said flock I traded among the soldiers, which 8 pesos I turned over to the Lord Governor; further, I collected six pesos in this *Villa;* I received from the Lord Governor a flagon of wine worth 10 pesos for the Monday and Saturday Masses; I received an *arroba* of wax worth thirty-seven pesos and 4 *reales;* I collected in this *Villa* of Santa Fe twenty-four pesos which I turned over to the Father Guardian; further eight pesos more which were spent to [increase, or knead?] it.

(e) Minutes, I f.

f.1   In this church of the *Villa* of Santa Fe on the Third day of the month of October of Seventeen Hundred and Seventeen, the brethren of the Confraternity of Our Lady of the Rosary together see it fitting that Bernardo de Sena[115] be elected as *Mayordomo*, which they carried out and declared with the Reverend Father Guardian, Fray Francisco de Yrazábal, presiding, naming as deputies: Sebastián Gonzales, Antonio Montoya, Miguel Sandoval, and Andrés Montoya; and

---

114. *Arroba:* A Spanish weight of twenty-five pounds.

115. More often called "Bernardino," having been named in baptism after the Italian Franciscan preacher, St. Bernardine of Siena. Born in Tezcuco, Mexico, he came to New Mexico in 1693 with the *"Españoles Mexicanos"* when he was nine years old. In 1705 Bernardino de Sena married Tomasa Martín Gonzales, and after her death married Manuela Roybal. By 1728 he had acquired much real estate in Santa Fe and the Cuyamungue Grant. He not only was the most active and devoted *Mayordomo* the *Conquistadora* ever had, but also served for years as Syndic of the Franciscans.

that it may so appear the said Reverend Father Guardian signed it, and those who knew how, leaving as deputies for the outside [communities] the above-mentioned.

> Fray Francisco de Yrazábal
> For Sebastián Gonzales
> Fray Francisco de Yrazábal
> Antonio Montoya
> For the *Mayordomo*
> Fr. José de Narváis Valverde
> For Andrés Montoya
> Fr. Carlos Delgado
> Before me,
> Miguel de Sandoval Martínez
> Deputy and Secretary

f.1v In this Church of Our Holy Father St. Francis of the *Villa* of Santa Fe, on the Second of October of Seventeen Hundred and Eighteen, the assembled Brethren of the Confraternity of Our Lady of the Rosary, located in said Church, re-elected in the Name of the Lord as *Mayordomo* of said Confraternity Bernardino de Sena, basing their decision on the experience which they have of his devotion and attendance, his punctuality and faithfulness, the Father Guardian, Fray Francisco de Yrazábal, assisting at said election, and they named as deputies: Sebastián Gonzales, Antonio Montoya, Sr., Miguel de Sandoval, Antonio Montoya, Jr. And that it may so appear they signed it with the Father Guardian on said day, month, and year.

> Fray Francisco de Yrazábal
> Antonio Montoya
> Antonio Montoya
> For the *Mayordomo*
> Fray Francisco de Yrazábal
> For the Deputy Sebastián Gonzales
> Miguel Tenorio de Alba
> Before me
> Miguel de Sandoval Martinez

(f) Accounts, 2ff., f.63 and f.97

f.63 Likewise, the Reverend Father Guardian, Fray José Guerrero, received seventy-five pesos from the dues of el Paso which Baltasar Trujillo handed in; another eleven pesos from La Cañada which Tomás Núñez handed in;

The account having been settled, of the Saturday and Tuesday Masses of the Confraternity of Our Lady *La Conquistadora* of the Rosary, and Feast of the Purification, and Masses for deceased members from the Eleventh of December of 1716, with the Reverend Father Guardian, Fray José Guerrero, its dues amounted to a hundred and one pesos, which the Confraternity has paid until today, the 21st of June of 1717. And his Paternity has received a hundred and thirty-seven pesos, by which he still owes thirty-six pesos.

Because of the absence of General Juan Páez Hurtado,[116] *Mayordomo* of the Most Holy Virgin in her Confraternity of the Rosary, I, Fray José Narváiz Valverde, took charge of the Confraternity since the Tenth day of July of this year of Seventeen Hundred and Seventeen, in order not to miss the Masses and Fiestas until a *Mayordomo* is elected.

The Convent remained owing 36 pesos to the Confraternity; the deputy of La Cañada handed in two bushels of wheat which were given to the Reverend Father Fray Francisco Yrazábal; further, one pair of woven understockings. The three Fiestas arranged for at 18 pesos apiece, and thirteen Saturdays at two pesos, and twelve Mondays at one peso, the whole amounts to ninety-two pesos. On the Third day of the month of October of 1717, I, Bernardo de Sena, was elected *Mayordomo* of the Illustrious Confraternity of Our Lady of the Rosary. I paid the Convent six pesos mentioned above which were owed it; further, I gave the Reverend Father Fray Francisco de Yrazábal, Guardian, 40 pesos on the Confraternity's account on the 16th of October of this year. To haul wheat from La Cañada I paid four pesos to Salvador de Archuleta;

f.63v　further, I gave Salvador de Archuleta six pesos for hauling the wheat which he brought from La Cañada; to the Master Juan de Medina for a job in the chapel of building the High Altar, and building a Sacristy, sixty pesos; for the sung and low Masses for five brethren who have died, twenty pesos; six pesos for the three Masses for a brother who died in La Cañada, because the two low ones were not said at one peso, but at two pesos; I paid the Father Guardian for the two feasts of December and February, and the Saturday and Monday Masses, ninety-six pesos, so that I am paid up until now the day of settlement, which was the Twenty-third of March; and the Padre still owes one peso for the future; those paid are fifty-six pesos, and with the above-mentioned 40 they amount to 96. Further, I have given Andrés Montoya twenty-two pesos for fetching the lumber to build the sacristy; I gave Andrés Montoya 8 pesos for the help in getting the lumber; the account of pesos for lumber is closed, which are thirty; and twenty *vigas;* and to Salvador de Archuleta I gave twenty-two pesos and four *reales* for fifteen *vigas* more. I handed in ninety-two pesos to the Reverend Father Guardian, Fray Francisco de Yrazábal; another twelve pesos which I paid for [the Masses of] the deceased brethren; another twelve pesos which I paid for three deceased brethren, as it will be evident from the bills; Ninety-six pesos which I have spent on beeswax for all the festivities and Masses of the year; thirty pesos which I handed in to our Father Guardian on the 22nd

---

116. See note 113.

day of September; sixteen pesos' worth of beeswax for Our Lady—
f.97 I took out in the year of Twenty-four, thirty-five rams for the
Father Guardian, Fray José Guerrero; two castrated lambs and
one ram; I further took out for the said Father Guardian in this year
of 1724, for the month of December, twenty rams; with five more for
said Padre; in said year and month I took out forty-five old sheep,
since I knew they would die, and I sold them for money to the soldiers
at the Palace; I took out fifteen rams on February 5, 1725, for the
Father Guardian; on June 3 of the same year I took out fourteen
rams for the Father Guardian, Fray José Guerrero; in the month of
October of the year 1725 I went out and took from the flock of Our
Lady two old sheep, which were going to die this winter, and ten rams
for the Father Guardian; in the month of December I took out 28
rams which I turned over to the Father Guardian; further, on June
12 of the year 1726 I turned in to the Lord Governor 40 rams which
I took out of the flock of Our Lady; further, in said year on the
20th of the month of October I turned in 44 rams to the Father Guardian from the flock of Our Lady; and four goats—
f.97v Today, the 1st of June of 1717, the *Conquistadora* Virgin, and her
Confraternity, has three hundred and eight sheep in the flock of
the General Don Felix Martínez,[117] which were placed in the care
of Juan Gonzales—
I, Bernardo de Sena, received three hundred and eight sheep,
which are in care of Juan Gonzales, of the Confraternity of Our Lady,
and among them are forty rams which I brought away, because the
said [Gonzales] told me they were prejudicial to his flock and asked
me to leave just enough for breeding purposes. Of the said rams I
have given thirty to our Father Guardian for the Masses, and the
other ten I sold for beeswax. Examining said flock I took out ten of
the oldest heads, which one could see would die this winter, which the
said Juan Gonzales turned over to me, and which I sold for nine pounds
of beeswax.
When the Lord Governor and Captain-General, Don Antonio Valverde, left me, Bernardo de Sena, in his place [as *Mayordomo*], I went
out to examine the flock of the Confraternity of Our Lady of the
Rosary, and I counted three hundred and eighty-two. And from said
number I took out fifty rams and twenty old ewes. . . .

THE END

---

117. Martínez was also interim Governor, and probably *Mayordomo* of the Confraternity around this time.

APPENDIX

LA CONQUISTADORA FRAGMENTS

(Archives of the Archdiocese of Santa Fe, Spanish Period, No. 1)

(a) Inventory, 9ff., f3-11

Digo Yo el Capn Alonso del rio maior domo del a cofradia de *f3*
nra señora/ La Conquistadora que resevi todo lo contenido, de
alagas y cosas per/ tenesienes a dha, Cofradia del mre de canpo
franco Gomes robledo/ maior domo que fue de dha, Cofradia
en el año de ochenta y/ cuatro y reconosiendo Por memorias
y resivos que tiene da/ dos el Rdo Pe Por fray franco de Vargas
ministro presidente/ del Rl de san lorenso, que se le deve, de
la cofradia ochenta y/ cuatro pesos de dho año de ochenta y
cuatro que no alcanso la/ Limosna, en el tienpo de dho maior
domo franco Gomes robledo/ mas en todo lo demas digo que lo
resevi fiel y legalmente,/ sin faltar, alaga alguna La cual funcion
de entriego se/ Yso ante el Pe Por fray franco de Vargas
ministro/ presidente del Rl de sn Lorenso, asistiendo juntamente
el/ alfez franco Lucero de godoy, y Pedro Ydalgo y el alfez blas
griego/ secretario y diputado de dha Cofradia y por que conste
en todo/ tienpo Lo firmo dho Pe, maior domo, del año de ochenta
y cuatro/ en beinti y seis dias del mes de febrero, del *año* de
ochenta y sinco—

  frai fran.co deVargas   franco Gomes
                Robledo Alo deL Rio
  Franco Matteo
  Lucer d odoy
  Po ydalgo   . Ante mi sro—
                  Blas Griego

En este Rl. de Sn. Lorenzo en dies, y ocho dias del mes de otubre/ *f3v*
del año de ochenta y seis Visito Nro. R.do Pe. fray Pedro Gomes
Pre./ Vice Custto. y Jues Ecclesiastico Ordinario de estas Proas
de la Nueva/ Mex.co Las alaxas y ropa de Vistir de la Reyna
de los Angeles, La Con/quistadora; Cofradia que esta fundada
en este dho. Rl. y aviendo Vis/to y re conosido todas las alaxas
contenidas en la memoria de atras hallo/ Su Pd. Rda. algunas
cosas indesentes pertraidas y biexas, todas las quales/ dio por
consumidas, Mandando Su. Pd. Rda. que de la ropa que se
pudiere/ aprovechar, para algun ornamento, o casulla, se aga,
o se aplique para/ otra cosa nesesaria del alino de la Reyna de
los Angeles, y asi mismo/ si se pudiere comutar alguna alaxa
o alaxas Se pueda aser, aplicando/ la limosna para otros gastos
de dha Cofradia; y aviendose liquidado/ todo lo que ay el dia
de oy en ser, y que pueda servir con desencia, Se hizo,/ La
memoria Siguente_____/

YMagenes

Primeram.te La echura de Nra. Sra. La conquistadora, de bara,
de/ alto poco mas, de bulto_____/
Mas un santo Sxpto, de bulto de bara y media en alto_____/
Mas un Niño Jesus de bulto de poco mas de media bara_____/
Mas tres Liensos de bara y media de alto; el uno de Nra. Sra.
de Guada/lupe; y el otro de Nro. Pe. Sn. Fran.co: y el otro de Sn.
Antt.o____/ Mas un Niño Jesus de bulto de un xeme de alto____/

79

Mas una Ymagen deel Sagrario. (*This last entered later in a different hand.*)

Joyas

Primeram.te un biril pequeño de oro____/ Mas, sinco laminas de carei pequeñas____/ Mas, quatro Agnus de abalorio____/ Mas, otro ReliCario de Sn. Diego, de cobre sobre dorado____/ Mas, una Rosa de plata sobredorada Con sinco piedras____/ Mas una Crus de feligrana pequeña____/ Mas tres pares de sarsillos, unos de perlas y oro, y los otros dos pares de pla/ta sobredorado con sus piedras, unas berdes, y otras encarnadas____/ Mas, una Gargantilla de perlas de quatro hilos, con un cordero, de oro____/ Mas, otra de quatro hilos de perlas____/ Mas otras dos de alxofrar, La una de seis hilos Con una Crus de plata y la/ otra de sinco; Con su crusesita de oro; Con sus relumbronsitos____/ Mas otra gargantilla de alxofrar de tres hilos rebueltas con corales____/ Mas otra gargantilla de nuebue corales gruesos, y Cuentas doradas____/ Mas, un rosario de corales gruesos engarsado Con casquillos de plata/Sin crus____/ Mas otro rosario de pexi____/ Mas, Una roza de plata, quebrada____/

Se dio por consumida para un clavo de Na. Sra. y una rosita de filigrana—

Bestidos

Primeram.te Un bestido de lama blanca Con su galon de oro, y fluequesillo/ encarnado aforrado en asul____/ Mas un bestido de lanpazo de flores, Con punta de plata y oro, aforado/ en lienzo encarnado____/ Mas otro bestido berde de razo Con punta de plata aforado en lien/sesillo asul____/ Mas otro bestido amusgo de flores, Con punta de oro, aforrado en/ mitan encarnado____/ Mas otro bestido de media lama con flores asules y el campo blanco/ con punta de oro, aforrado en mitan colorado____/ Mas otro bestido encarnado con franxin de oro, aforado en mitan asul____/ Mas dos sayas, una de chamelote pardo; y la otra de razo asul____/ Mas quatro Tocas; una de oro y seda de dos hilades, con puntas de lo mismo____/ Y dos de pellexo de culebra, y otra de red____/ Mas, otras dos tocas blancas, de espumilla; y un pañuelo____/ Mas, una saya negra de capichola, aforada en liensesillo asul____/ La saia negra se dio por consumida aplicandola para que se aga una manga para la crus. (*This last entered later in a different hand.*)

f4

Consumido Consumida— Por orden de N P. fr F.co de Vargas Jues eclesiastico ordinario q se mejoraron en unas andas

Mantos

Primeram.te un manto asul de razo bordado con oro y plata; en florones____/ Mas otro de das mas co asul, Con sus puntas de plata____/ Mas otro de tafetan berdoso, Con sus puntas de oro____/ Mas otros dos de razo blanco, llanitos____/ Mas otro manto azul de tafetan con sus puntitas de plata____/ Mas otro manto negro de seda, Sebillano____/

Camisas

Primeram.te siete camisas Con sus balonas labradas de distintos/ colores____/ Mas otras dos de Cambrai; llanitas____/

Bestuario de las andas

Primeram.te un bestuario de las andas de razo blanco, bordado Con ber/de____/ Mas otros bestuarios de las andas negro de bayeta de castilla____/

Palias

Primeramente una palia de ruan, labrada de asul____/ Mas,
otra palia labrada con rozado____/ Mas, tres plumeros, de plumas
finas____/

Alaxas y ropa del S. to Xpto:

Primeram.te tres sabanas, de ruan con sus puntas____/ Mas,
Una colcha morada de lama, de flores, aforada en tafetan plate/
ado____/ Mas otra colcha de tafetan asul con sus puntas de
plata____/ Mas, otra colcha de sayasaia blanca____/ Mas, sinco
halmuadas de seda; dos bordadas, y Lustres con sus en/caxes
____/ Mas, otra halmuada de ruan, labrada Con seda naranxada
y asul/ Mas, una funda de mitan amarillo____/

Ropa del Niño

Primeram.te una tunica rozada Con su soga y su corona____/
Mas dos Camisas de cambrai____/   no las ay—
Mas otra Camisa de cañutillo____/ Mas, otra Camisa de red____/   f4v
Mas un bestido de tela blanca; aforado en tafetan asul____/   x
Mas otro bestido dechorreado, encarnado____/ Mas, otro bestido,   x
de razo berde, Con los calsones de razo encarnado____/ Mas una   x
bandera de lama blanca Con su crus de bidrio asul y sus casqui/
lles de plata____/ Mas dos bestiditos del niño de Sn. Antt.o, y
tres camisitas____/ Mas un belo de tafetan asul, con punta de
plata____/ Mas otro de tafetan asul llanito____/ Mas, otro belo
de liensesillo asul con sus flueces____/ Mas, una Culebra de red,
de hilo de la tierra____/ Mas, Un Niño de bronze de poco menos
de media bara;____/ Mas, Un baul en que se guarda la ropa___/
Mas, otra caxa de bara, de sedro____/ Mas, otra caxa grande,   Se consumio
esta caxa se consumio por estar echa pedasos (*This entered by*   esta caxa por
a different hand, the same as on marginal note.)   orden de Nro. R.do Pe fr;
Todas las quales partidas, asi como van expesificadas, le fue/   Pedro Gomes
ron entregadas al Mayordomo, Alonzo del Rio; para que en/   Vice Custt.o
todo tiempo sea obligado a entregarlo, segun i como se contiene   de esta S.ta Custta:
en/ este libro, advirtiendosele que si pusiere alguna mexora o
aumento/ lo ponga con toda expesificasion al pie de este auto,
menos listones____/ o sintas, por ser cosa manual y poderse con
fasilidad perder; pues aun/ que puede suseder dar algunos
listones o sintas de limosna los cofra/des al tiempo que se les
cobra; puedan expesificarse al tiempo de/ las quentas, o de
entregar el dho. mayordomo a quien le susediere/ y se le dan
las grasias por lo vien que a obrado, y el aseo conque/ tiene las
cosas de la Cofradia; asi lo proveio mando y firmo____/ Su Pd.
Rd;a en dho: dia mes y año. *ut supra.*
fray Pedro Gomez
Vice Custt.o y Jues Eccless:o

Ante mi
Fray Joseph Spi.la
Secrett.o y Nott.o Appco

Aumentos que a puesto el mayor domo en la Cofradia este Año
de/ Mill, Seis cientos y ochenta y siete años____/ Primeram.te
un bestido de chamelote asul, que dio el Sargen/to Mayor Roque
Madrid____/ Mas una corona de plata que dio fran: Luzero a la
Reyna de/ los Angeles de limosna siendo Mardomo el Capp.an
Alonzo del/Rio____
Visitose este libro en que estan asentadas todas las cosas perte-/
necientes al culto y aliño de la Reyna de los Angeles la/

f5

Conquistadora y esta todo fiel, y legal segun sus partidas todo con/ aseo, y limpiesa de todo lo qual se le dan las graciàs por el cuydado, y/ fomento que ha tenido en todo lo perteneciente a dha cofradia/ y juntamente ayer tenido algunos aumentos que ensu tiempo/ an dado de alaxas como vestidos algunos viene-chores/ y se le encarga en lo de adelante no falte al fomento de/ dha cofradia solisitando las limosnas acostumbradas po-/niendo con claridad de quien las da y por que en todo tiempo, conste lo firmo su Pd Rda en catorze dias deel mes de Abril/ de mill seicientos, y ochenta y siete en este Rl. y Villa de San Loren/ço por ante mi el infra esp.to notario.

Fray Nicolas lopes   fr. Xptoval Daza
   Custodio, i Jues   visenotario apostolico
   ecclesiastico

En nuebe dias del mes de Junio, de millseiscientos y ochenta y ocho años puso de/ aumento un vestido de raso blanco labrado fran:co Lucero de Godoi, siendo mayordomo/ el sarx:to mayor Alonço del Rio____/ Mas unos sarsillos de perlas falsas, y espejuelos, y un espejito pequeño con serquillo/ de estaño____/ Mas otro bestido de raso berde labrado que dio fran:co Lucero, para el niño Js de bronce/

Aplicose a
San Miguel
este vestido—

Visitose este libro en que se asientan todas las cosas, y alaxas pertenesi-/entes a Nra: señora la conquistadora, y esta fiel, y legal. segun sus par-/tidas, todo con aseo, y limpiesa de todo lo qual se le dan las gracias por el/ cuidado, y fomento que a tenido en todo lo pertenesiente a la cofradia, y/ juntam.te de los aumentos que en su tiempo an dado, y se le encarga en/ lo de adelante no desfallesca, ni desmaye en el fomento de la cofradia, so-/licitando las limosnas acostunbradas, poniendo con claridad quien las da, y/ por que conste lo firmo su R:a dose dias del mes de Agosto, de mill seis/cientos y ochenta y ocho años, en este Real de S. Lorenço, por ante mi el in-/fra scripto notario____

fray Pedro Gomez   Antemi
Vice Custt.o y Jues Eccless:o   fray Antt:o de Azevedo
                                       Nott:o Appco

f5v
No vale,
borrado—

Sertifico yo fr. Diego de Chabarria como a tenido la/ Cofradia de Nra Sra del Rosario gasto de veinte, i quatro ps/ en sera toda la qual sera se a gasto en las festibidades de/ Na Sra a costa de su maiordomo Alonso del Rio todo lo qual/ me consta doi esta sertificasion oi miercoles dos de fe/brero de ochenta, i nuebe——
fr. Diego de Chabarria
(*The above entry crossed out with a few oblique strokes.*)

Visitose este libro en que se asientan las cosas, y alaxas per-tenecientes a Nuestra Señora la/ Conquistadora, y esta fiel, y legal segun sus partidas todo con aseo, y limpiesa, de todo lo qual/ se le dan las gracias por el cuydado, y fomento q a tenido en todo lo perteneciente a la co-/fradia, y juntamente de los augmentos, q en se tiempo an dado, y se le encarga en lo de ade-/lanto no desfallesca, ni desmaye en el fomento de la cofradia solicitando las limosnas;/ y porq algunas cosas no sirven ya para el ministerio a q eran destinadas, se ordena/ al mayordomo de dha cofradia, q unas naguas de chamelote musgo aforradas en mitan/ morado, de Nra. S. a se den por consumidas, y de ellas se hagan unas caydas pa las andas/ y una corona de relumbrones con flores de oro; y algunos listones se hagan ramilletes/ pa la dicha Ymajen de N.a S.a aplicando tambien pa las andas unos retasos de ruan la-/brado; y se dan por consumidos unos cacles del S.to Xto: assi lo proveyo, y mando N. R.do/ P.e fr. Fran de Vargas Pre.or Custodio, y Jues Ecclesiastico ordinario de la Sancta Custodia de la/ Conversion de S. Pablo de la Nueva Mexico en veynte y tres de Mayo de mil seyscientos, y/ ochenta y nueve años por ante mi el infrascripto notario____

frai fran.co deVargas
Custt.o y Jues. Ecle.co

Antemi
Fr. Augustin de Colina
Notario Apostolico

Visitando Nro R.do Pe fr. franco de Vargas P.or Custto i Jues Eclesso ordinario de estas/ Provincias, i Reino de la nueba Mex.co este Libro de las alajas pretenesientes a La/ Cofradia de Nra Señora la conquistadora en este Real de San Lorenso allo su/ Paternidad no faltar cosa alguna, reconosiendo sus partidas por este libro; si,/ mando su Pad al maiordomo de dha cofradia fuese consumida una saia/ negra de Raso aplicandola a una Cruz manga, como asi mesmo una cruz/ pequeña, i una Rosita de feligrana para que de ella se aga un clavo para la/ corona de Nro S.ra y aviendosele echo cargo al maiordomo diese las/ quentas ante nos, juntamente con sus diputados, Reconosio Su Pad mui/
Rda las memorias, i Libros enque se asientan los cofrades, f6 i echos cargos a *dho*/ maiordomo del numero de los co-frades que stan asentados, i de lo apersebido/ de las limosnas, i sus gastos de cofradia, Reconosimos faltar la limosna de al-gunos/ de los Cofrades; presentando el *dho* maiordomo sus descargos, i en ellos el/ uno es estar ausentes muchos de los Cofrades de este Reino, aqui nos satisfico con/ sus proprias memorias, i declaro lo que en su poder actualmente pasaba de/ limosnas que son siento i quarenta i un pesos, pagado por mano del sindico/ al Pe Por fr Joseph Spinola almonasi ministro de dho conVto del/ Real de San Lorenso quienes declararon ser asi verdad; i a pedimento de *dho*/ maiordomo, i Cofrades Re-presentaron a su P R se isiese libro nuebo de/ asiento de cofrades, a que reconosio su P. por el dho libro, i pedimento ser mui/ conveniente el que se aga libro nuebo asentando los Cofrades que actualmte/ se allan en este Reino, i de estos los que dan, i acuden con su limosna cada un/ año para que *dho* maiordomo de sus quentas en lo de adelante, sinq'/ pueda faltar por esta dili-gensia el que se acuda con vigilansia a la utili/dad y bien de las almas de los cofrades Vibos, i difuntos, para que sea/ La Justisia distributiba, i gosen todos de los divinos sufragios, i por recono-ser/ su P M R el trabajo solicitud, i esmero conque el *dho* maiordomo, i diputados/ de *dha* Cofradia solicitan aumentarla, le damos las grasias de lo bien/obrado promentiendonos en lo de adelante se esmeraran en no faltar/ aeste mandato, asi los que los son actualmte como los que fueren en/adelante, asi lo proveio mando, i firmo su P R en catorse de Maio de mil sei-/ sientos, i noventa, i un años por ante mi el infra scripto secrett.o i Notto Appco____/ y juntamente mando su P R que se guarde el libro antiguo, i lo firmo en/ dho dia mes i año ut supra____

fray franco deVargas
Custodio, y Jues Ecclco

Ante mi
Fr. Antto Guerra
secrett.o i Notto Appco

En treinta dias del mes de Nove de millseiscientos y novta y un años,/ puso de limosna el Alferez franco Luzero de Godoi un

vestido para/ La Virgen ss.ma de primavera de china, o raso
labrado que lo mas es encarnado,/ con su____ (*illegible*) del
mesmo genro____ siendo ma/yordomo el sargento maior franco
de anaia Al/mazan____

f6v Mas una tunica de belillo blanco que dio de limosna una Co/frada
llamada Juana de aleman
Visitando N.R.P. fray Joachin de Ynojosa P.r Vice Custodio,
y Juez Ecclesiastico ordinario destas/ prov.as y Reyno de la
Nueva Mex.co reconosio este libro donde se asientan las alajas
de la Co-/fradia: y aviendo visto: q ay algunas cosas q segun
lo decretado por el S. to Officio no deben ponerse a/las Ymajenes;
mando su P.d R.da q no se les pusiessen a las Ymajenes; sino
q de las tocas, y camissas/ se hagan unas palias, y de los vestidos
del niño Jesus, se appliquen a otras cosas de su culto; y las/
quentas, perlas, y joyas se dan por bien applicadas al sagrario
del S.mo Sacramto, quedando/ siempre el dominio de ello a la
Cofradia de N.a S.a la Conquistadora: el sombrero se dio por/
consumido, y de las plumas q se hagan ramilletes: y el vestido
verde de raso labrado del/ niño Jesus se applico a la Ymajen
de S. Miguel. Y por q.to Mayordomo, y Diputados de/ esta Cofradia representaron tener derecho a una lampara de plata, q
estaba en el Conv.to/ del Socorro por ser de dha cofradia se les
entrego, con un vaso de plata sin pie: por no aver/ asta aora
cosa en contrario: y se les applico una diadema de plata, por
una corona de plata q/ dicen se perdio, q es de la Cofradia: y
para mejor govierno de dha/ Cofradia, y q los omissos en las
limosnas, no piensen gozar los suffragios, sin ayudar/ como deben
a la Cofradia,__ mando su P.d R.da q en faltando tres o quatro/
años arreo alguno o algunos de los Cofrades: pida el mayordomo
al P.e Mro/ Guar.n deste Conv.to del real los amoneste en pub-
lico; y de no emmendarse, se/ borraran de la memoria del libro,
y q no gosen de los suffragios acostumbrados; y lo/ mismo pedira
a los PP.s Mro.s de los demas Conv.tos deste reyno: y enq.to a
las limos-/nas atrasadas; se requiedra a los Podatarios ausentes
de las limosnas: y las limos-/nas q se recobraren de los años
pasados, siempre se expresen con distincion; para q de/ todo
conste en la visita. y el libro viejo; q esta indecente: trasladados
ya los Cofrades/ se quemara: y enqto al presente mayordomo el
Sarjento mayor Christoval/ de Tapia, y Diputados se le dan
muchas, y repetidas gracias por los augmentos/ y puntualidad
conq a obrado: encargandole de nuevo prosiga en su fideli/dad,
q pagara la reyna de los Angeles Ntra. S.a por los servicios de
su culto./ assi lo proveyo, mando, y firmo su P.R. en primero
de Septiembre deste año de mil seys-/cientos, y noventa y dos
años ante mi el infrascripto Secret.o y Nott.o Appco____
Fr. Joachin de Ynojosa
Juez Eclesiasthico   Antemi
                                   fray Augustin de Colina
                                   Secrett.o y Nott. Appco

f7   Una Lampara de plata qe Se saco del nuebo Mex.co que para/
ba en el Conv.to del Socorro. que se bolvio a esta Cofradia por/
ser suya____/ Mas una diadema de plata, la qual era pertenesiente al/ Conv.to del Passo. Y se comuto por una corona de
plata, que era/ desta Cofradia____
eL maestre de capo, y teniente gelar Luys Granillo, mayordo/
mo de la Cofradia de nutra, S.a del rosario. Ju. del rio. franco/
Jurado y Jua pacheco. y Christobal de garamillo, diputados/ y
pedro ydalgo, secretario, decimos y certificamos/ q recebimos

las alajas todas segun y como dejan la / memoria de este libro,
es cepto, lo qe el auto antece/dente, de nutro R-do pe bici Custto
fr-Jachin de/ Ynojossa dio por consumido en la bisita/ y por
q- coste, lo firmamos los qe saben firmar/ en biynte y tres del
mes de mayo de mil ceyscien/tos y nobenta y tres años.

luis granillo   Pedro Hydalgo
  Ju pacheco   Ju del Rio   secretario

Augmentos que a puesto el teniente Gl. deste R.o luis granillo/
desde el año de nobenta dos y tres, asta el de nobenta y sinco;
en q salio/ electo Maiordomo el Sr. Gor y Cappn G.l D Diego
de bargas Sapata Lu/xan Ponse de leon y por su teniente Maior
domo, y Diputado/ Maior dicho Teniente G.l Luis Granillo____/
Primeramente un ornamento de damasco de chin, amarillo, y
blanco,/ que consta, de Casulla, estola, manipulo, frontal, pano
de caliz y bolsa de/ corporales; prosedido dicho ornamento de la
limosna de una piesa (?)/ yndia que dio el Sr. Gor____/ Mas,
siete candeleros de asofar____/
Mas, un farol, de oja de lata, y bidrieras, grande____/ Mas, una
barilla de Hierro de dos baras, para la cortina de N S.ra/ Mas,
un dosel grande, de tafetan doble, encanado, y amarillo que/
sirbe de baldoquin, el cual dio el Sr. G.or de limosna,/ Mas dexo
dies y seis candelas de sera____

Marginal notes: Mas se gastaron trese pesos en recaudo para dicho ornamentto—13 ps. Mas seis ba ras de bandi lla q le sirbe a nuestra Señora una caja grande con su sera dura y un cajonsito dentro f7v

Augmentos del año de 95

Primeramente, dos candeleros de plata que dio el Sr. Gor Maior
Domo de la Cofradia de N.S.ra____/ Un bestido de brocatto azul
de primavera aforrado en/ tafetan encarnado____/ tres baras
de toledo encarnado____/ quatro baras y media de colonia encarnada todo para/el dho Vestido____/ Una camisa de cambrai
con encaxe____/ Mas un sitial [?] de seda de Blanco, verde y
amarillo____
digo yo el Capn Antt montoya teniente de mayordo/mo juntamente con los diputados y el escribano que/ resebi del teniente gl
Luis granillo Las alajas todas/ segun y como resan en este libro
Y para que conste/ Lo firmamos en quinse de abril deste año de
mil/ Seis Sientos y nobenta y Sei____

Antto de Montoya   Luis Martin   Sebastian Gonsales
                                        Antte mi
                          Antt Luzero de godoy
                      secretario de dicha Cofradia

Digo Yo el Capn D. Alonzo que como Te/niente de maiordomo
de la madre de Dios/ Resebi de el Capn Antonio montoia las/
alajas siguientes____
Primeramente nuestra Señora La conquis/tadora con bestido y
ornamento corona/ de Plata y Un agnus y Un biril y Rozario/
Mas el niño Jesus con Una cruz en las ma/nos y Una banda y
Supeana Plateada/ Mas otro niño de bronze____/ Mas Un Jesus
nazareno de lienzo____/ Más nuestra Señora de el Sagrario de
lienzo____/ Mas nuestra Señora de la Soledad, de lienzo____/
Mas nuestra Señora de los Remedios en anta Pintada____/ Mas
nuestra Señora deel Rozario en el guion____/ Mas otro niño
Jesus de madera____/ Mas Una lanPara de Plata____/ Mas Un
farol de Vidrio____
Mas seis candeleros de Plata cuatro chicos y dos grandes____/
Mas onze candeleros de bronze____/ Mas ocho Vestidos y con el
que tiene/ Puesto La Virgen son nuebe____/ Asi mesmo Resevi
toda la rropa/ que perteneze y es de la birjen San/tizima y Para

Marginal notes: f8   f8v los pequeños son de la Ygla y no son mas

de dos de la
Cofa.

que conste lo/ firme con los diputados en/ tres de febrero del
año de 1697 a—
Alphonsso Rael de Aglar
Antto Monttoya
A rruego de Sebastian Gonzales
Joseph de Contreras
A rruego de Luis Martin
Joseph de Contreras

f9

Digo yo Sebastian gonzalez theniente de mayor-/domo que rrezevi
en 3 dias del mes de Marzo de 1698/ de mano del Cappn D.
Alonso Rael de Aguilar las Ala/jas seguientes que son las per-
tenezientes A la Cofradia de nu/estra señora del Rosario____
Puso de aumento el Sr. Gov.or y Capp.n Genl D Pedro Rodriguez
Cubero lo/ siguiente./ Una corona de Plata sobre dorada imperial
esmaltada y guarnessida con/ piedras./ Mas, un vestido de bro-
cato encarnado con su manto azul del mesmo.____/
el S.or Gen.l D. Diego de Vargas dio un vestido raso labrado
azul/ y manto blanco. Y un frental blanco de tela, y una casulla
del mismo.
el mayordomo Sebastian Gonzales puso de aumento unos man-
teles/ y una palia Labrada con seda encarnada y doce candeleros.

Auto de
Visita:

En La villa de S.ta fee en treinta de Mayo de mill setes.tos y
dos años hacien/do su visita Jurica N.R.P. fr. Antt.o Guerra
P.or Cust.o de esta S.ta Custt.a de la/ convercion de S Pablo
y Juez Ecless.co ordinario por autoridad App.ca de este Reyno/
y Prov.as de la Nueva Mex.co & Mando su P. d R.da comparecer
a Sebastian Gonzales/ Bernal theniente de Mayordomo para que
diese las quentas de la limosna que/ de la Cofradia de Nra S.ra
La Conquistadora ha resevido. el qual comparecio/ ante su P. R.
con los libros de dha Cofradia, y registradas sus partidas/ se
reconocio haber pasado nueve años sin que se aigan tomado las/
cuentas, por cuia causa estan llenas de confusiones, y casi im-
posibles de ajustar./ Por tanto mandaba y mando Su PR. que
de aqui en adelante/ haga el dho Mayordomo un libro en que
con toda claridad y distincion/ hasiente lo que resiviere de
limosnas, y su distribucion y gasto—

f9v

Y cada quatro meses venga con dho Libro a este Conv.to de la
dha Villa y/ junto con el P.e Guardian de el (a quien concede
su PR. su autoridad para este/ efecto) se ajusten las cuentas,
y vayan firmadas de ambos para que al/ cabo del año quando se
hase eleccion de Maiordomo se hagan notorias/ a los Cofrades,
y se vea que se han enpleado sus limosnas en las misas/ fiestas,
y funsiones de Nra S.ra y en algunos augmentos, y les servira/
De consuelo, y se animaran los fieles a azentarse en tan S.ta
hermandad/ y assi mismo con esta diligencia el Prelado que
fuere en su Visita tendra/ menos que hacer, y si reconosiere
alguna omision en los maiordomos/ y diputados se excluiran de
poder exercer dhos oficios, y a los que fieles/ procedieren la Mag.d
Divina de Dios nro. Sr. Les recompensara con premios/ espiri-
tuales favoreciendolos como a siervos de la Reyna de los Angeles/
Assi lo proveyo mando y firmo su PR. en dho dia mes y año ut
supra ante mi el infra scripto notario____
Fray Antto Guerra
    Custto y Jues Eclesso
                                       Antemi
                            fray Miguel Muñiz
                            Nott. App.co

f10

En la Villa de sta Fee. En primero dia del mes de/ maio de mill
setesientos y quatro Yo el Cappn Ju./ Paez hurtado theniente

de Gov.R y Capp.n Gen.l/ de este R.no de la Nueba Mexco
Recevi Como Ma/yordomo de la Cofradia de nra ss.Ra la Con-
quista/dora de Sevastian Gonz.l todas las Alaxas perte/nesientes
a dha Cofradia Cuio tener es como se sigue/ Primeramte Un
vestido EnCarnado nuebo de tela Con/flores de oro guarnecido
Con galon de francia fino Corespon/diente a las flores de la tela
Con un manto de tela asul/ de flores de oro Con la misma guar-
nizn____/ mas otro Bestido de Raso de florencia asul Con flores/
de oro mui Ussado sin manto____/ mas otro Bestido de Raso
de florencia Con flores en/Carnadas Verdes y asules Usado y
sin manto____/ mas otro Bestido de lama Blaca Biejo Con un/
manto de Razo Blanco Con flores de oro guarne/sido Con un
galon falso de oro de un dedo de ancho____/ mas otro Bestido
de Razo amusgo Con flores de se/ da Blaca guarnesido Con Boto-
nes falso que sirve/ de orla Biejo y sin manto__/ mas otro Bestido
de Resaso de china Color de fuego lla/no Viego sin manto____/
mas otro Bestido Blanco de lanpaso Biejo guarne/sido con una
punta de oro sin manto____/ mas otro Bestido de lanpaso berde
sin guarnicion/ y sin manto mui ussado____/
mas otro Bestido de chamelote asul Con un manto/ asul Bordado f10v
Biejo____/ mas Una Corona de Plata dorada Con 25 Piedras/
falsas berdes asules y encarnadas Con su Crus/ Enssima____/
mas otra Corona de Plata llana Bieja____/ mas Unos manteles
de Ruan de Sinco Baras____/ mas tres Sabanas las dos de
morles y una de Ruan/ Con punta de lorena____/ mas Una
Colcha de lama de china morada guar/nesida Con una punta
Grande de Ylo de la tierra a/forada en tafetan berdoso____/
mas Un Coxin de tafetan sensillo negro mas otro de/ dho tafe-
tan____/ mas Un sudario de Bretaña Con punta fina____/ mas
Un anus Con Reliquias de diferentes santos de palta/ dorado
Viejo____/ mas Un Benadito de oro Con un Berueco____/ mas
Una Rosa Con sinco piedras de Plata dorada/ y las dhas Piedras
falsas Blancas asules y berdes____/ mas Unos Sarsillos chan-
Bergos de Plata dorada de fe/ligrana Con dos piedras asules
falsas y Dos Cala/basillas de christal y Cada Sarsillo Con dos
pendien/tes de a quatro perlas finas____/ mas otros Sarsillos
de feligrana de plata dorados Con Una higa de cristal Cada
uno____/ mas Un biril de oro esmaltado En asul Con quatro
pi/laritos En las Esquinas____/ mas Un Rosario de corales de
Siete misterios en
Garçado en Plata____/ mas otro Rosario de peje muier de siete f11
misterios____/ mas tres tunicas del niño Una morada otra
En/carnada y otra Blanca Biejas____/ mas todas las quales dhas
alaxas he Recevido/ Como dho es y para que conste lo firme En
dho/ dia Ut supra____
    Ju. Paez Hurtado

Assi mismo Una palia que dio a Nra s.Ra La con/quistadora La
Muger del negro tambor de Seda Ver/de y aguebada____/ Mas
Una Saya de chamelote Verde que dio a Nra/ ss.Ra Micaela de
Velasco que sirve debajo el bestido

f11v (Blank)

(b) Accounts, 1f., f20

Digo Yo frai fran.co deVargas, que resevi del S.or Mayordomo,/ f20
Alonso del Rio, y juntamente de los diputados, la limosna de/
siento i tres pesos i quatro tomines. a quenta de la cofradia de
Nra/ S.a la Conquistadora__ la qual limosna es aplicada en el/
S.to Sacrificio de las misa, por el vien de las Almas de los
cofrades/ de dh.a Cofradia, assi Vivos, como difuntos__ con

dixtinsion/ la dh.a limosna que ha enterado dh.o Alonso del Rio,
que fue pagar/ ochenta i quatro pesos que devia la Cofradia
en el tiempo del/ mayordomo antesesor, franco Gomes Robledo,
al qual no le alcansa/ron las limosnas por estar los Cofrades en
suma necesidad/ i no aber podido dar todos, y assi hechas las
exactas diligen/sias, por dh.o Mayordomo actual, entero dh.a
limosna i lo que/ en el tiempo que ha que tiene la cofradia a su
cargo, sin dever/me cosa alguna. Antes si Reconosco en lo que
he insperimen/tado lo haze con Caridad i Zelo, y Solicitud junta-
mente/ con los Señores diputados que le acompañan que cada
uno/ en particular se esmera al Servicio de la Serenissima
Reina/ de los sielos Maria Santissima __ Y para que [hole]
en todo/ tiempo conste este mi Resivo lo firme en ocho dias del
mes/ de Mayo del año de mill-Seisientos i ochenta i Sinco:____

frai franco deVargas

Digo Yo fray Joseph, de espindola Por y ministro pre/sidente,
deste RL. de sn Lorenso que resevi del Capn alonso/ del rio,
Maiordomo de la cofradia de la Reyna de los angeles/ La conquistadora, siento y secenta y tres pesos dende siete/ de Junio
Por las misas de los cofrades Bibos y difun/tos y juntamente
de los Cuatro festibidades de la Reyna/ de los angeles y pa que
en todo tienpo Conste di este junta-/mente Un resibo de doup,
del Rdo Pe fr Ju muñoz/ del tienpo que dixo las misas y por
berdad Lo firme/

f20v   En dos dias del mes de febrero deste presente año/ de ochenta
y seis____

fray Joseph, Spila

Digo yo fr Diego de Chabarria Por/Ministro pnte deste R.l de Sn
Lo/renso q Recebi del Cpn ALonso del Rio/ Maior domo de la
cofradia de Na Sra del Rosa/rio La conquistadora ochenta ps
dede trese de octubre/ Por las misas de los cofrades Vibos, i
difuntos y/ junta mente de dos fiestas q se an selebrado a Na
Sra/ La una de la consepsion, la otra de la purificasion y/ Para
qe en todo tiempo conste i este Resibo en/ dos dias del mes de
febrero de ochenta, i nuebe.

fr. Diego de Chabarria

f1
Cuaderno
Segundo en
beinte y dos
(fojas ?)

(c) Accounts, "Cuaderno Segundo," lf.

1689

Libro en que se asientan las limosnas que tiene de Recivo, la
Cofrad/ de Nra. S.a la Conquistadora: consta este libro de
veynte/ foxas comiensa este libro oy catorse de Junio de mil
seyscientos/ y ochenta, y nueve años____

Recivo de las limosnas de la Cofradia.

Primeramente el S gor y Capn gl dn domingo Jironsa/ dio de
Limosna tres Candelas de Sera en tres ps__03ps/ nuestro mui
reberendo pe Custodio frai/ franco de bargas dio Unas medias
en un p__01p,/ dio de Limosna el gl dos ps de Jabon__2p,/
diego arias un pso de Jabon__02p/ el Sarjento maior franco de
anaia ma/yordomo de La reina de Los angeles dio/ de limosna
por si y por su esposa dor pares__/ de medias en dos ps__02ps,/
doña Jasinta de quiros unas calsetas en un pso 02ps/ ynes de
tapia dio de limosna un pso de Jabon__01ps/ Josefa barba dio
un pso de Jabon__01p/ franco romero de pedrasa dio de limosna/
por si y por su esposa Un Campeche en Cuatro ps dos por este

año y dos por el pasado__04ps/ el Capn po de Sedillo dio de
Limosna un carnero en un pso__01ps/ Chrisptobal tapia unas
calsetas en un pso__01ps/ Jua de balensia su mujer dio unas
me/ dias en un pso__01ps/ pablo el biejo Cuatro gallinas, en un
pso__01ps/ doña Luzia barela de Losada dio de li/mosna dos
baras de liston encarnado__02ps/

Por la de la buelta____V 21ps   f1v

Pago angelina dos pares de medias finas/ en cuatro ps__04ps./
Pago el ayudante antt.o lusero. unas/ Pulseras de abalorio negro
y perlas/ falsas en dos ps. por ssi y por su esposa__02ps/ Pago
pedro de leyba por si y por su es/possa. de la limosna. unas
medias blan/cas de lana. y unas calsetas de blanco. y negro. que
sumontero [?]: son dos ps.__02ps./ el padre comiss.o fr. Ju.o
muños pago/ por su limosna una candela de sera en un Ps.__
01ps./ Pago nro. Padre fr. diego de mendosa su li-/mosna en una
candela de sera en un peso__01ps./ Pago Ju.o holgin su limosna
en quatro/ gallinas en un ps.__01ps./ Pago estevan turibarba
su limosna/ quatro gallinas en un ps.__01ps./ Pago fran.co
fresqui su limosna Por si y/ por su muger un carnero y una
borrega/ de año cada cabesa en un ps. son dos ps.__02ps/ Mateo
lucas g.or de las ysleta pago su limosna/ en un carnero de año
en un ps.__01ps./ Pago su limosna el padre fr. Antt.o de asebe-/do
una candela de sera en un ps.__01ps./ Ambrosio fresqui pago su
limosna en u-/nos Sapatillos en dos ps. por si y su muger__02ps./
Pago Ju.o garsia. por si y por su muger/ deste presente año. su
limosna. y del año/ Pasado. de ochenta y ocho. dos baras de/
brtana en quatro ps.__04ps./ Pago diego de Luna su limosna una
libra/ de chocolate en dos ps. por si y por su esposa__02ps.____
45ps.

(d) Accounts, 4ff., f1-f4.   f1

Pague ael Rev.do P.e fray Lucas Arebalo 6ps./ por qta de las
missas de los Lunes en un azadon__V 06p/ mas pague ael R.do
fr. Ju. mings, 4pos. por las/ missas del cap.n Ju. de Dios luzero
de godoy__V 04/ mas llebo el Rev.do P.e fray lucas, dos gamussas
pr./ las missas de los Lunes de cofradia y un manojo/ de tabaco
__V 06p/ Resevi del P.e fray lucas 6 pesos__006/ Resevi del
Capitan montoya de bernalillo, 3 carne/ros, y tres de Ju. gonzales,
que resibio el P.e Guardian 12p/ resevi de la limosna de los
Cofrades de Nra Señora/ del Paso 13 pesos con Ant.o tafoya__
013/ en 13 de Agosto, resevi de los diputados de la Yll.e Co/fradia
de Nra señora del Rosario treynta pesos año/ recoxieron en dho
dia__30/ Yten resevi una bela de zera en Un peso__01/ Yten
resevi dos pesos, en unos zapatos__02/ Yten resevi, quatro
carneros__08/ en 4 de Septiembre resevi del diputa/do Diego
marquez quatro pos__04/ en dho dia resevi del Capitan Vargas
quatro pesos__04/ mas tres pesos de la mosonga, y el cantorsito/
bartolo__03/ en 4 de septi.e resevi dos pesos__02/ en 10 de 7.e
resevi sinco pesos__05/ en 11 3 pesos__03/ en 15 resevi dos pesos
de Ju. de leon__02/ en 24 resevi 4 pesos__04/ en 26 resevi dos
pesos__02/ en 2 de octu.e resevi dos pesos__02____118
en 18 resevi dos pesos__2/ en 22 resevi dos pesos__2/ en 28 resevi f1v
del Capitan Roybal, tres antas delgadas, y una/ gorda, dos cueros
de zibolo, y dos pares de zapatos y un pso de xabon__25/ en 29
resevi dos pesos__02/ mas resevi del Capitan Diego Montoya 4
pesos__04/ en 3 de nob.e resevi dos pesos__02/ en 9 de Dic.e
resevi unos zapatos__02/ en dho dia una gamusa__02/ en 12 de

dho unos zapatos__02/ en 13 resevi onse fan.s de trigo de la
canada__44/ asi mismo resevi seis p.os de una fan.a de haba, y/
alberjon que resibio mi comp.e el barbero, y me los/ a de abonar
en palacio__06/ mas dos p.os de Ant.a de mansanares__02/ mas
resevi dos fan.s de trigo de nicolas griego por la viuda de archuleta que coxi yo por el flete de mi ca/rreta__08/ (*This entry
crossed out*) en 22 de hen. resevi dos pesos__02/ en 3 de feb.o
resevi tres pesos__03/ en 28 de marzo de *714* resebi quatro pesos
__04__212__/ mas resebi una apachita que Vendi en 67 p.os/
para pagar al rev.do P.e gu.an las missas, y fiestas de/ la co-
fradia__067____219/ Yten, resevi el año pasado de 713, de la
limosna de/ los soldados Cofrades, sesenta y sinco pesos, que pa/
gue ael Señor Gov.or por quenta de Ciento y beinte/ y dos en
que la dexo empeñada el marquez de/ La peñuela el tiempo que
fue mayordomo__065/ Yten resevi este año de *714* de la limosna
de/ los soldados cofrades, con algunos que se asentaron

f2   de nuebo, ciento, y seis pesos, y de ellos pague/ al Señor gov.or
sinq.ta y siete, con que se acabe de pa/gar los Ciento y beinte y
dos del marq.z y tiene/ La Cofradia en ser en palacio quarenta,
y nuebe pesos/ oy 17 de marzo de 1714__49p/ mas resevi del
Paso onse pesos de xabon__11/ mas dos velas de a 6 en libra/
mas resevi de alburquerque seis carneros__12/ mas resevi de
Balthasar Truxillo de la limosna/ del Paso quinse pesos en sayal
que abone en pala/cio__15/ mas abone en palacio onze pesos, y
seis que cojio/ mi muger en dos pares de zapatos y una bara/
de Crea que hasen *32* Con la partida de arriba__17/ mas resivio
el rev.do P.e gu.an fray Ant.o Camargo de la limosna de alBurquerque ocho pesos en 4 car/neros__8/ mas entregue ael Rev.do
P.e fray Joseph guerrero/ onze pesos de xabon y dos baras de
bretana/ de la limosna del Paso__15/ mas resevi un peso de
xabon__01/ mas resevi treinta y dos pesos de la limosna de/
nuestra señora, que estan en palacio__32/ mas resevi de los
Cofrades de san Buena Bentura nuebe reses, a Catorse pesos
los e dado/ mas de otra res de san Buena Ventura que mato/
el frayle en el Camino e resevido 4 pesos, y los de/mas sabe mi
Comp.e Ju. Garcia quien los de/ve__mas resevi de mig.l de la
Cruz quatro pesos__04

f2v En l.o de febrero de *715* resevi de la limosna de la cañada/ dies
fanegas de trigo__40/ mas ocho costales y m.o de mayz__12-6/
mas unas calzetas de hilo de algodon en 3 pesos, y dos pares de
guantes__05p/ mas dos pesos de tomatitos__que coji yo, y devo
a la cofradia/ mas resevi quarenta y un pesos en *17* de marzo/
de *1715* de la limosna de la Villa__4p/ mas resevi quatro pesos
de rosa xiron__04/ mas resevi de salvador de archuleta tres
pesos de/ xabon, y de tomas nuñes quatro pesos de xa/bon, y
dos manojos y m.o de tabaco__12/ mas resevi quatro pesos de
la limosna de la vi/lla (*viuda*?) del xeco, y su suegra__04/ mas
resevi dos pesos de tomatitos de andres de archuleta__02/ (*This
line crossed out*) mas resevi dies pesos de mi compe el barbero en
xabon y tabaco__10/ resevi un manojo de tabaco de mateo
Truxillo__02/ resevi otro de montes de oca__02/ resevi de ant.o
montoya el moso 3 pes__03/ resevi de las limosna del paso quarenta y un/ pesos en zera a 4 pesos libra__41/ en *1o* de mayo de
715 resevi 4 pesos de xabon__04/ mas 3 pesos de Ju. de Rivera
de puxuaque__03/ mas resevi del capitan Ju. Gonsales de la
li/mosna del rio abajo tres carneros, y una borega/ tres gamu-
sillas de a peso, las dos y una de dos pes/ quatro pares de medias,
y uno de guantes__21/ mas resevi dies y siete pesos de la limozna
de/ la villanue.a en antas, y trapillos____17

Mas Rezevi de la limosna de Bernalillo dos pares/ de Juantes en **f3**
2 p__02p/ Yn __ tengo que cargar de la limosna de los pre/sidiales
del año pasado de *715* y *716* yncluien/do en dha limosna 100p
de una Apacha Que/ Se Rifo por haverla dado de limosna a nra
S.a/ Como quinientos y Sinqta ps y de ellos tengo es/ Cripto A
Mexco pidiendo Un Corateral para/ el Maior adorno, de la s.a__/
Yten resevi del P.e fray mig.l muñiz dipu/tado del Rio abajo seis
pesos de la cofradia__6/ Yten resevi quatro pesos de la limosna
de la cañada__4/ en 6 de Junio rezevi ocho p.s de la limos/na de
los Cofrades de Alburquerque 8-/ en 8 resevi quatro pesos en
un palio y/ unos zapatos de la limosna de albur/querque__04/
resevi sinco carneros de la limosna de albur/querque y Bernalillo
__10/ Yten resevi dos pesos de salv.or de archuleta__02/ Yten
resevi del P.e fray mig.l Una ga/musa, y unos guantes de la
limosna/ de bernalillo__03/ Yten resevi un carnero del P.e fray
mig.l__02/ Yten resevi *28* p.os de 7 fran.s de trigo de la/ Cañada
__16/ Yten resevi *16* pos de quatro fan.s de trigo/ de la cañada
__16/ Yten resevi una sarta de chile en 2p__02/ Yten rezevi
quatro pes de Bernardo de Sena__04__
Yten resevi de la limosna del paso seten/ta y sinco pesos con bal- **f3v**
tasar Truxillo__75/ Yten otros onse pesos de la limosna/ de la
cañada__11__
En tres dias del mes de octubre de mill setecientos, i dies i siete/
años, entre por Maiordomo de la Cofradia de nra s.ra de/ el
Rosario, yo Bernardo de Sena, i he resevido lo sigui/ente.__
Resevi del Diputado de la Cañada Tomas Nuñes sesenta/ i
quatro ps. que recojio de los Cofrades de N.tra s.ra en Trigo, i
chile,__064/ el dia *10* de octubre sali con los diputados a recoger
la limos/na en esta Villa de s.ta fe, i se secojieron Siento, i diez
i siete p.s__117/ Mas recoji otros beinte ps. en esta dha. Villa__
020/ Mas resevi del diputado del Passo el Sargento Christoval/ Data ojo
Truxillo, diez i siete ps. en sera p.a el gasto de la Cofradia__017/ ―――
Mas dos ps. que pagaron en dos bs. de toledo__002/ Mas resevi 17—
siete ps. en sayal, q di al P.e Guardian__007/ Ajustado todo lo
Resevido Ynporto quinientos y onse p__00511/ Mas Resevi 40
carneros del Cappn Juan Gonzales de Nra S.a/ q tiene Nra
S.a__ en el a de *1718*__080/ Mas otras *10* obejas biejas de dho
a__020/
Empesando Yo dho mayordomo el año de *1719*, resebi/ lo siguiente, En dies y nuebe de octubre, del año pasado/ de *1718*
Resebi del diputado de la Cañada, thomas nu/ñes, siento y beinte
pesos en trigo y chile__120/ mas otros 8 pesos en dos fanegas de
trigo del dho tomas nu/ñes__008/ mas recoji en la Villa de s.ta fe
y rresebi, sesenta y nuebe/ pesos__69/ mas Recoji, treynta y Data ojo—
ocho en dha Villa__38/ Resebi en palasio de cuenta de los señores 75
soldados/ 75 pesos en una arroba de sera__75/ mas rrecoji otros ―――
ocho pesos, en cuatro sartas de/chile__08/ mas tres pesos de ojo—
liston que resebi los quales/ se gastaron en Rosas para N.a Data
S.a____V929__
Mas (*torn*) tres pesos que entregue al Ro Pa/Guardian__mas **f4**
otros quatro que Resebi y los qui/te en papel para N.ra S.a para Data ojo
un libro__/ Resebi siete pesos de el diputado de el passo/ Xptobal 04
Trugillo en sera__07p/ Resevi de el diputado el Rio abajo el Data ojo
dia *17*/ de myo *1719* an *40* ps en carneros y medias y Cabras/ ―――
Mas Resevi 2 p de guebos__42/ 07
Recebi en palacio ciento y treinta y ocho ps que costo el palio Data ojo—
__138/ 138
Mas Recoji en la Villa de Stta fee disinuebe ps/ en sera__19/ ojo—
Mas Resevi otros dies y seis pesos q recogi en la dha Villa__16/ ―――
19

Mas resevi en dha Villa siento y trese pesos q Recogi de los
Cofrades/ de dha Villa__113/ Mas resebi de el diputado Juan
Gonsales siete p.__07/ Mas Resevi Por quenta del SR GovernR
Dn Antto Valberde/ En la Cañada Siento y seis p.__106/ Mas
Recogi en la Villa sinquenta y dos p.que le/ Entregue Al Señor
GovernR__52/ Mas le entregue Al SR Govern.R Sesenta y cuatro
p que/ yse de las borregas biejas y lana que rezevi__64/ Mas
Resebi en esta Villa tres anegas de trigo que/ le entregue A
Joseph Antt fernandes por quenta/ del señor Govern.R y quedo
Una__12/ Mas Resevi ocho p del diputado Ju Gonsales en el/
Rio abajo__8/

Data ojo—
30
Mas Resevi por quenta del S.r GovernR dies libras de zera/ q
las quales se gastaron el dia de nuestra S.a de la puri/ficasion
____Ynporta treinta p__30__V 424

f4v
Data ojo—
113
Mas Resevi Una aRoba y media de zera Para el gasto/ del a. la
qual me la dio el SR Govern.R Ynporto siento/y trese ps y cuatro
Reales__113-4/ Mas Resevi del SR GovernR Sinco Varas de Ruan
que/ se pusieron en las bentanas de la Capilla de nuestra s.a/
y una piesa de sinta q Ynporta todo dose p__12/

Data ojo
10
Mas Resevi Un frasco de bino q me dio el SR Govern.R/ para las
Misas de los sabados y lunes__Ynpto/ dies ps__10/

Data ojo—
24
Mas ocho libras de zera que me dio el S.R Govern.R/ las cuales
Ynportan beinte y cuatro p__24/

Data ojo—
18
Mas gaste disiocho p en tres hermanos difuntos. que se les dixeron
las misas como costara por los bales__18/ Mas Resevi dies
Carneros que saque de los sincuenta/ que saque del ganado de
nuestra S.a y entregue/ Al Pe Guardian fr. franco de Yrazaval,
y los cua/renta que Resevi entregue a coris que fue por quenta/
del SR GovernR y beinte borregas que Resevi de/ dho ganado
comulte entre los soldados y los qua/les ps entregue al SR

Data ojo—
10
Govern.R__140/ Mas Recogi en esta Villa seis p__6/ Rezivi del
sR Govr Un frasco de Vino en 10 p para/ las misas de lunes y

Data ojo—
37-4
savados__10/ mas rezivi una a de zera en treinta y siete p y n__
37-4/ Mas recoxi en esta Villa de Stta fee beinte y/ quatro p que

Data ojo
le entregue al padre Guardn__24/ Mas otros ocho p que se xas-
taron en añidrirla____V 394__

(e) Minutes, lf.

f1
En esta Yglesia de la billa de Santa fee/ en tres dias deel mes de
otubre de mil/ setecientos y desisiete asi Juntos los herma/nos
de la Cofradia dee Nuestra señora deel/ Rosario tienen A bien
que de por mallordo/mo elecpto Bernardo de sena lo qual/ ysieron
y pronunciaron precidiendo el/ rbendo padre guardian frai frnco
de y/rasabal nombrandose por diputados/ A sebastian gonsales
Antto montoya/ Miguel de sandobal y Andres/ montoya y para
que Conste lo firmo dho rebendo pa. guardian y los que supie/ren
degando por diputados de afuera/ los anteriores__

Fray Franco de Yrazabal

Por Sebastian Gonsales
Fray Franco de Yrazabal

Anttonio mon
toya

      Por el Mayordomo
      fr. Josef De Narbaiz
            Balverde

      Por Andres montoya
      fr. Carlos Delgado

      Antte Mi
Miguel de sandobal martines
diputado y secretario

En esta Yglecia de N S P Sn Franco de la Villa de Sta Fe en f1v
dos/ de octubre de mill setecientos, y diez y ocho años, Juntos los
Heros/ de la Cofradia de N Sa del Rosario fundad en esta dicha
Yglecia, reeligi/eron en el nombre del Sr por mayordomo de
dicha Cofradia a/ Bernardino de Sena fundados en las experi-
encias, que tienen de su de/vocion, y asistencia, puntualidad,
y fidelidad, asistiendo a dicha elecion/ el Pe Guardian fray
Franco de Yrazabal, y nombraron por Diputados/ a Sebastian
Gonzales, y Antto Montoya el Viejo, Miguel de Sandobal, Antto/
Montoya, el Mosso, y para q conste lo firmaron con el Pe Guar-
dian/ en dho dia, mes, y año

Fray Franco de Yrazabal   Por el Mayordomo
           Fray Franco de Yrazabal
Antton- montoya   Por el diPutado Sebastian gozales
Antt.onio montoya   Miguel Thenorio de Alba
      Antte mi
    Miguel de sandobal
      Martines

(f) Accounts 2ff., ff63 and 97.

         Por la de enfrente__51p/ f63
Yten resivio el R. do P.e gu.an fray Joseph/ guerrero setenta
y sinco pesos de la limos/na del paso, que entrego balthasar
Truxillo__075/ Yten otro onse pesos de la Cañada que en/trego
thomas nuñez__011____137__/
Ajustada La q.ta de las missas de los saba/dos y martes de la
Cofradia de nra Señora/ La Conquistadora del rosario, y fiesta
de la/ purificazion, y missas de difuntos Cofrades/ desde onze
de Diciembre de 716 an. con/'el Rev.do P.e gu.an Joseph
guerrero in/porto su limosna Ciento y un peso, paga/da La
Cofradia hasta oy 21 de Junio de/ 717__Y tiene resevidos su
pat.e Ciento, tre/inta y siete pesos, con que queda devien/ do
treinta y seis pesos__036p/
Por la auciencia del Gen.l Ju.o Paez Hurtado Mayordomo de la
ssma/ Virgen, en su Cofradia del Rossario, tome a cargo yo
fr. Joseph Narbaiz/ valverde la Cofradia, por que no falten las
missas, i fiestas hasta que se elija/ Mayordomo, desde el dia diez,
del mes de Jullio de este año de mill sete/cientos i diez i siete__/
Quedo debiendo el Conv. to 36 p.s a la Cofradia__036ps/ Entrego
el diputado de la Cañada dose fanegas de Trigo, que se le/ dieron
al R. P.e fr. Fran.co de Yrazabal__048/ mas un par de calcetas
de ilera__002ps/ Ajustadas las tres fiestas a 18 p.s cada una, i
trese Sabados a/ dos p.s__ i doze Lunes a peso, monta todo
noventa, i dos p.s__092ps/ con que deben al Conv.to solo seis
p.s__/
En tres dias del mes de octubre de 1717 años, fui yo Bernardo ojo—
de Sena/ electo Mayordomo de la Yll.e Cofradia de nra s.ra de
Rossario__/ Pague al Conv.to Seis p.s q se le debian aRiva
mensionados.__0006/ Mas di al R.P. fr. Fran.co de Yrasabal
Gu.an en 16 de octubre/ de este año 40 ps. a quenta de la Cofradia
__0040ps./ Para condusir Trigo de la Cañada pague a Salvador
de archuleta/ quatro ps.__0004 ps./
Mas di a dho. Salvador de Archuleta, seis ps. de acarreo de f63v
acarreo de Trigo/ que traxo de la Cañada__0006ps/ Mas al
Maestro Juan de Medina, por una obra que se ofrese en la ca-/
pilla, de lebantar el Altar Mayor, i hazer Sachristia sesenta ps.
__060ps/ Mas de las Misas cantadas, i resadas de sinco herm.os
que han muerto/ beinte ps.__020ps/ Mas de un h.o q murio en

là Cañada de las tres misas seis ps. porque/ no se dixeron a p.o
las dos resadas, sino a dos ps.__006ps/ Ma pague al P.e Gu.an
de las dos fiestas de Diziembre, i febrero/ y las Missas de Sabados, i lunes noventa y seis ps. con que quedo/ pagado asta el dia
del ajuste, que fue beinte i tres de marzo,/ i quedo el P.e deviendo
un peso p.a adelante./ son sinquenta i seis ps. los pagados, i con
los 40 de arriba son 96__096ps/ Mas tengo dados a Andres Montoya beinte i dos ps. para la/ saca de la madera p.a hazer la
sachristia__022ps/ mas le di A andres montoya 2 ps. para la
ayuda de la saca de la madera__2ps/ se ceRo el numero de los
pesos, de la madera que son treita__30/ y Beinte bigas y A
Salvador de Archuleta le di Beitidos p./ y Cuatro Reales por
otras quinse Bigas__22ps.4R/ entregue al R.o P.a Guardian frai
franco de/ yrasabal nobenta y dos pesos__92/ mas otros dose
pesos que pague por seis her/manos difuntos__12ps/ mas otros
dose pesos que pague por otros hermanos difuntos como constara/
por los bales__12/ mas nobenta y seis pesos que gastado en/ sera
para todas las festibidades y/ misas deel año__96ps/ mas treinta
pesos que entregue a nuestro/ padre guardian el dia 22 de septi/
embre__30ps/ mas dies i seis pesos en sera para nuestra/ Señora
16p___310p2__

f97 Saque el ano de veinte y cuatro doze carneros/ para el P.e guar-
dian__ *(This entry crossed out)*/ Mas saque este año de veinte
y cuatro treinta y sinco Carneros para el P.e/ Guardian fr.
Joseph Guerrero__35/ mas dos castraditos y un carnero__03/
mas saque para el dho P. guardian ente año de/ *1724*__ por el
mes de Dize. veinte carneros__020/ con mas sinco para el dho P.e
__005/ mas en dho año y mes saque quareta y sinco/ borregas
biejas por conozer ze avian de morir y/ las bendi a los soldados
pr dinero en palazio__045/ mas saque quinse carneros a *5* de
febre/ro de *1725*. para el padre guardian__015/ Mas *3* de Junio
de dho año sage catorze carneros para/ el pe. Guan fr. Joseph
Guerrero__014/ fui el mes de otubre deel año de *1725* y s/aque
no vale deel ganado de nuestra s.a cuarenta *(last word crossed out)*/
y dos obejas biejas que se abian de mo/rir e este ynbierno y dies
carneros pa/ra el padre guardian__032/ Saque el mes de diziembre del dicho a/ño *23* carneros que le entregue/ al pa.
guardian__28/ mas entregue en *12* de Junio del año/ de *1726*
al Señor GovR *40* carneros que/ Sa que deel ganado de nuestra
señora__40/ mas entregue dho año a *20* deel mes/ de otubre *44*
carneros al P.a Guardian/ del ganado de nuestra Señora__44/
y cuatro cabras__04

f97v Oy *21* de Junio de *1717* años tiene la/ Virgen Conquistadora y
su Cofradia/ en el gañado del gen.l D.n feliz martines/ tre-
cientas, y ocho ovejas que se dieron/ apartido a Juan Gonzales__
Resevi llo bernardo de sena tresientas y ocho ca/besas que estan
en poder de Juan Gonsales/ de la Cofradia de N.ra S.a y entre
ellas/ quarenta Carneros los quales trugue/ Porque me dixo el
dho le eran de per/gucio en el ganado que degase los que/ se
abian menester para padres de los/ dhos carneros tengo entre-
gado A nues/tro padre Guardian treinta en quen/ta de las misas
y los otros dies bendi/ por sera__ Registrando el dho gana/do
Saque dies cabesas las mas biejas/ que eChaba de ber se abian
de morir/ este ynbierno las quales me entre/go el dho Juan
Gonsales Las cuales bendi/ por nuebe libras y media de zera__
Abiendome dexado en Su lugar el SR Govern.R/ y Cappn Gral D.n
Antt Valberde; A mi Bernardo/ de Sena: fuy A Reconoser el
ganado menor de/ la Cofradia de nra S.a del Ros.o y conte
tresien/tas y ochenta y dos. Y de Dha cantidad saque/ sinquenta
Carneros y beinte borregas biejas

Nihil Obstat:
Rev. Fr. Roger Huser, O.F.M., J.C.D.
Censor Librorum

Imprimi Potest:
Very Rev. Fr. Romuald Mollaun, O.F.M., S.T.D.
Provincial Minister
July 2, 1948

Imprimatur: ＼
Most Rev. Edwin Vincent Byrne, D.D.
Archbishop of Santa Fe
July 4, 1948